FAMILY HISTORY
WEB DIRECTORY

FAMILY HISTORY FROM PEN & SWORD BOOKS

For more details see www.pen-and-sword.co.uk.

FAMILY HISTORY WEB DIRECTORY

*The Genealogical Websites
You Can't Do Without*

JONATHAN SCOTT

Pen & Sword
FAMILY HISTORY

'Good gracious a Darracq!'
For Genevieve

First published in Great Britain in 2015
and reprinted in 2016 by
PEN & SWORD FAMILY HISTORY
An imprint of
Pen & Sword Books Ltd
47 Church Street
Barnsley, South Yorkshire
S70 2AS

ISBN 978 1 47383 799 7

A CIP catalogue record for this book is
available from the British Library

Typeset in 10pt Palatino by Mac Style Ltd, Bridlington, East Yorkshire

Printed and bound in England
By CPI Group (UK) Ltd, Croydon, CR0 4YY

Pen & Sword Books Ltd incorporates the Imprints of Aviation, Atlas,
Family History, Fiction, Maritime, Military, Discovery, Politics, History,
Archaeology, Select, Wharncliffe Local History, Wharncliffe True Crime,
Military Classics, Wharncliffe Transport, Leo Cooper, The Praetorian Press,
Remember When, Seaforth Publishing and Frontline Publishing.

For a complete list of Pen & Sword titles please contact
PEN & SWORD BOOKS LIMITED
47 Church Street, Barnsley, South Yorkshire, S70 2AS, England
E-mail: enquiries@pen-and-sword.co.uk
Website: www.pen-and-sword.co.uk

CONTENTS

INTRODUCTION

I've been writing about genealogical websites since the tail end of the 1990s. As the fresh-faced assistant editor at *Family History Monthly*, it was my duty to check and polish the 'Web Wise' column. This was always a highlight of the working week, as it meant going up to the third floor – the location of the one computer in the building with dial-up Internet access.

Today I have my very own computer, with which I continue to visit genealogical websites, from one-man labours of love to global behemoths. Over the years, the market leaders have taken on personalities for me. I see Ancestry as an eager know-it-all with all the latest gadgets. Genuki is a grand but faded uncle with a pencil moustache. TheGenealogist is an intrepid explorer with obscure and surprising knowledge. MyHeritage is a charming but overbearing American with a distressingly firm handshake. The National Archives is a raconteur, unaware of her beguiling beauty. And FamilySearch is a matronly aunt with an encyclopaedic memory.

To help you get the best from this cast of characters, and their lesser-known cousins, there's a filing system at work in this book. Each chapter lists websites broadly in order of importance, interest and usefulness. The idea being that for those just starting their research into a particular branch or topic, this will lead them quickly to the best or most interesting resources. Then in the index at the back, all the websites appear again, often more than once, but listed this time alphabetically by title, content or subject.

Each entry runs as follows: title, address, description (if warranted).

In many cases the address and title tell the whole story, so further explanation is superfluous. Some have names and addresses that obviously relate to the subject of a chapter, but where this isn't the case, more information has been added to the titles to make their relevance clear.

At other times the title I have chosen will be the content of a specific page, rather than the parent website. For example, perhaps we stumble upon a website called 'Aunty Em's Remembrances', but within this we find a surname index to Argyll newspapers between 1869 and 1901. In such a case the website's title is 'Argyll newspaper index, 1869–1901'.

Finally, with sites that appear frequently, I list both the specific page and parent. So a National Archives guide to researching coalminers becomes: 'Coalminers research guide, The National Archives'.

Fans of the old 'www' or 'http' prefixes may notice their absence from the majority of web addresses in this book. This is because most websites no longer need them to function properly. I have included them where required.

Web addresses change frequently. With so many websites listed, inevitably some will slip out of date. If you find a dead link, enter the title of the webpage, or the address itself, into your search engine of choice and hopefully you'll find it soon enough. If the website has completely disappeared you can try typing the address into the Internet Archive's 'Wayback Machine' (archive.org).

My only other piece of advice is this: make notes, either digital or physical. If you don't leave a trail of breadcrumbs, sooner or later you'll end up going round in circles.

I really hope you find this book useful. If you want to praise or complain you can find me on Twitter: @thejonoscott.

Section 1

FIRST STEPS

1.1 Getting Started

There's lots of help and guidance for budding researchers. Key lessons that come up again and again include: 'start from what you know', 'never assume' and 'write it down'. This chapter covers some of best 'how to' guides, plus the most useful starting points for first-steps research.

FamilySearch
familysearch.org/learn/wiki/en/Main_Page

The sheer wealth of information available through FamilySearch means that while the homepage is ever being simplified and streamlined, the experience can still feel overwhelming – especially if you have a common surname. For that reason I recommend a little background reading via the above Research Wiki. Then you can click on the homepage, register, and begin recording what you know; or you can go straight to search, and trawl the vast quantities of free census or parish data. There's also this getting started page: familysearch.org/ask/gettingstarted.

The National Archives
nationalarchives.gov.uk

Click on Find Guidance > Looking for a Person, and you're presented with the A–Z of TNA research guides. If you already know enough about your family to choose a relevant guide – such as an occupation perhaps – they're a great route to quickly understanding what information you will need to confirm before you can find out more. There's also the Start Here page (nationalarchives.gov.uk/records/start-here.htm), which details what they have/don't have and what's online/not online.

Why the Census is Helpful, Findmypast
findmypast.co.uk/content/expert-searching-census

All commercial websites have getting started guides – usually weighted towards persuading you to peruse their own collections or use their online tree builders. But there's still useful information and guidance to be had – this Findmypast page is a clear and simple introduction to understanding the census.

UK BMD
ukbmd.org.uk

Excellent hub to online transcriptions of UK births, marriages, deaths and censuses, plus other indexes/transcriptions of parish material, wills, MIs, and so on. Click on Local BMD, for example, and there are links to all county websites offering online transcribed indexes to the original GRP records held by the local register offices.

ScotlandsPeople
scotlandspeople.gov.uk

Click the Help and Resources tab and choose Getting Started to read a tailored guide to Scottish research. The site itself hosts BMD indexes, parish records and census records, plus other material held by The National Archives of Scotland. Free to search with a pay-to-view download system.

FreeBMD
freebmd.org.uk

When starting out, it's likely that you will be attempting to fix information about life events of the recent past. Step forward this project, which aims to transcribe the civil registration birth, marriage and death indexes for England and Wales from 1837, and provide them free online.

GOV.UK
gov.uk

Will tell you what you need to know about ordering copies of birth, death and marriage certificates. Unfortunately this only delays the inevitable moment when you will have to return to the actual GRO ordering service (gro.gov.uk/gro/content/certificates/default.asp).

Federation of Family History Societies
ffhs.org.uk/really_useful_leaflet.pdf

This link takes you to the 2014 edition of the Federation's getting started PDF guide, *Our Really Useful Information Leaflet*. It has a host of links and there's also a directory of member societies – information also available from the FFHS homepage.

Free UK Genealogy
freeukgenealogy.org.uk

Parent website of the aforementioned FreeBMD and its sister initiatives: freereg.org.uk (free baptism, marriage and burial records from parish/nonconformist registers); and freecen.org.uk (free census information from the years 1841, 1851, 1861, 1871, 1881 and 1891).

Research Forms, FamilySearch
familysearch.org/learn/wiki/en/Research_Forms

Free printable forms to help you organize your work. These include pedigree charts in various formats, plus forms specifically designed for noting information from particular sources – such as census material.

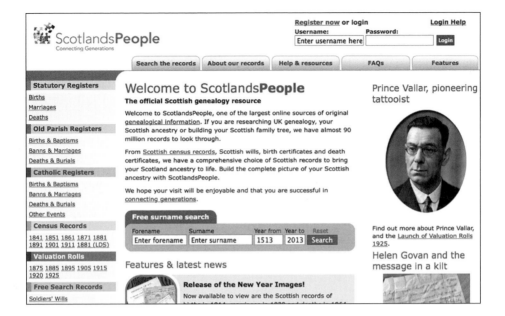

Genealogy Software Compared, Wikipedia

en.wikipedia.org/wiki/Comparison_of_genealogy_software

Simple article that compares the leading client-based genealogy programs on the market. A companion guide to web-based software is at: en.wikipedia.org/wiki/Comparison_of_web-based_genealogy_software.

FamilyTree

family-tree.co.uk/category/free-guides

From FamilyTree's mini-guides section, with bite-sized introductions to BMD records, parish registers, the census, online research, newspapers, trade directories and army records.

Genuki

genuki.org.uk/gs/

UK and Ireland Genealogy is a stalwart of genealogy online, and this is its starting out page. It may not look like much, but it's got it where it counts.

Commonwealth War Graves Commission

www.cwgc.org

The Debt of Honour Register is a database of individuals who died during both world wars. It also has details of the 67,000 Commonwealth civilians who died in the Second World War.

Society of Genealogists

sog.org.uk/learn/help-getting-started-with-genealogy/

SoG guides to various common sources and records, which explain their context and use, plus dates covered, indexes, finding aids and more.

UK GDL
ukgdl.org.uk

Genealogical Directories and Lists on the Internet provides links to all kinds of sites providing online databases, indexes and finding aids.

Forebears
forebears.co.uk/england

Attractive federated search hub launched in 2012, through which you can search datasets held by various commercial websites.

Cyndi's List
cyndislist.com/free-stuff/getting-started/

Explore getting started tools and advice as listed on the leading genealogical links site.

Get Started, BBC Guide
bbc.co.uk/history/familyhistory/get_started/

Concise introduction from a mothballed section of BBC History.

UK MFH
ukmfh.org.uk

Links site which brings together online databases and finding aids for military research.

Rootsweb
rootsweb.ancestry.com

An immense genealogical cooperative.

Getting Started, Ancestry
ancestry.co.uk/cs/uk/gettingstarted

British Genealogy Network
britishgenealogy.net

About.com, Genealogy
genealogy.about.com

Federation of Family History Societies
ffhs.org.uk

Getting Started, PRONI
www.proni.gov.uk/index/family_history/family_history_getting_started.htm

Archives for Family History, Archives Wales
archiveswales.org.uk/using-archives/archives-for-family-history/

GenesReunited
genesreunited.co.uk/contents/familyhistorygettingstarted

TheGenealogist
thegenealogist.co.uk

Getting Started: Genetics for the Genealogist
genealogyblog.com/?p=33208

To Pay or Not To Pay? A Guide to Choosing Genealogy Sites on the Internet
bbc.co.uk/history/familyhistory/get_started/paying_for_research_01.shtml

A Gentle Introduction to GEDCOM
tamurajones.net/AGentleIntroductionToGEDCOM.xhtml

Guide to Primary, Secondary and Tertiary Sources
lib.umd.edu/tl/guides/primary-sources

MyHeritage
myheritage.com

FamilyRelatives
familyrelatives.com

Deceased Online
deceasedonline.com

192.com
192.com

1.2 GRO Indexes

You've gathered together family papers, interviewed family members, and pencilled dates into a tree. Now it's time to start checking your facts through the GRO (General Register Office) registers. Civil registration of births, marriages, and deaths has been in place in Scotland since 1855, and in England and Wales since 1837. The civil registration indexes are generally referred to as GRO indexes.

ScotlandsPeople
scotlandspeople.gov.uk

Gives access to official records of births, marriages and deaths in Scotland – starting in January 1855 when civil registration replaced the old system of registration by parishes of the Church of Scotland. The statutory births index, for example, contains the indexes to civil registers from 1855 until 2012 (images of births from 1855 to 1913 are available to view). Click Births, Marriages or Deaths from the top-left of the homepage to find out more about the history of the system and the kind of data recorded – all three provided extra details in the first year, which proved too difficult to sustain in the long term.

FreeBMD

freebmd.org.uk

This is an ongoing project to transcribe the civil registration index of births, marriages and deaths for England and Wales, and provide them free. The system started in 1837 and is one of the most significant resources for genealogical research. You'll find index information from that year up to 1983, but it's not complete – you can check a breakdown page that shows progress by event and year.

UK BMD

ukbmd.org.uk/local_bmd

The Local BMD section has links to county websites offering online transcribed indexes to original GRO records held by the local register offices. Meanwhile at ukbmd.org.uk/gro_bmd there are links to websites offering online transcribed indexes based on the secondary data held by the General Register Office.

Certificate Ordering Service, GRO for England and Wales

gro.gov.uk/gro/content/certificates/

Whatever index source you use, once you have the GRO reference number you can order a certificate online via the Certificate Ordering Service. If you don't have the reference number you can still order a certificate, but it will take a little longer.

FamilySearch

familysearch.org/search/collection/2285341

FamilySearch includes the likes of this England and Wales Death Registration Index (1837–2007) courtesy of Findmypast. Again, to find out more, try the following Research Wiki page on civil registration in England (familysearch.org/learn/wiki/en/England_Civil_Registration).

BMDIndex

bmdindex.co.uk

Most of the commercial players give access to the GRO indexes in some form or another, but this facility from TheGenealogist team scores over its rivals, partly because of its simple three-months-for-a-fiver access deal.

Camdex

camdex.org

An example of a useful regional facility, this one covers Cambridgeshire. The material is based on the original registers – not the transcribed versions held by the General Register Office.

National Records of Scotland
nrscotland.gov.uk/research/guides/birth-death-and-marriage-records/statutory-registers-of-births-deaths-and-marriages

Guide to the statutory registers of births, marriages and deaths in Scotland.

Irish Genealogy
irishgenealogy.ie

Indexes of Irish GRO BMD back to 1864 and non-Catholic marriages from 1845.

Isle of Wight FHS
isle-of-wight-fhs.co.uk/bmd/startbmd.htm

Registered births, marriages and deaths on the Isle of Wight (1837–2010). An example of the kind of local source you may find via: ukbmd.org.uk/gro_bmd.

Civil Registration, Genuki
genuki.org.uk/big/eng/civreg/

Guide to civil registration in England and Wales.

GRONI, General Register Office Northern Ireland
nidirect.gov.uk/family-history

Access to Northern Irish birth, marriage and death records online.

Heir Hunter
hha-bmd.com

Upload and share civil registration documents with fellow researchers.

Scotland BDM Exchange
sctbdm.com

1.3 The Census

You've found your relatives in the GRO indexes, now it's time to read about them in the black-and-white snapshot of census night. Census returns open the door to new avenues of research. They allow you to find out about occupation, family, status, neighbourhood, community and more. This is where family history gets good.

Census, FamilySearch
familysearch.org/learn/wiki/en/England_Census

FamilySearch has a complete free index and transcription of the 1881 census. It also has free indexes to the remaining released censuses (1841 to 1911) for England and Wales, although you will probably need to consult a subscription website to see the full transcription online. This particular wiki page gives details of what each census recorded, plus advice about interpreting, and links to many external sources.

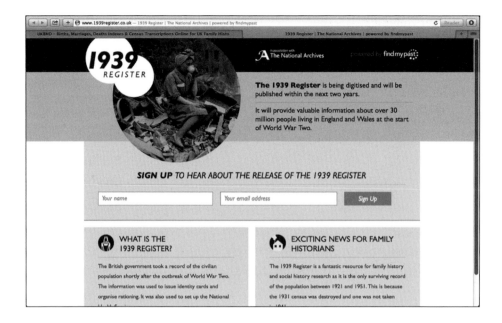

UK BMD
ukbmd.org.uk

Use the side menu to navigate to the page which lists sites that provide online transcriptions of census material. This includes major subscription sites plus all kinds of county hubs and small-scale local databases, sometimes compiled by individuals focusing on single villages or streets.

1939 Register
1939register.co.uk

This soon-to-be released register of more than 40 million Britons alive on Friday, 29 September 1939, was compiled shortly after the outbreak of the Second World War and was used to issue identity cards and organize rationing. It is the only census-like record of the population between 1921 and 1951.

ScotlandsPeople
scotlandspeople.gov.uk

The site hosts census returns for Scotland from 1841 to 1911. It costs £7 to search the census indexes, which includes thirty page-credits for viewing images of the original enumerator's pages. Images are in TIFF or JPEG format and cost five credits each.

TheGenealogist
thegenealogist.co.uk

Searches are conducted on a county basis using an address, placename, keyword, forename or surname; this requires a subscription of course, but you can volunteer to transcribe census records in exchange for search credits.

Census of Ireland 1901/1911
census.nationalarchives.ie

Search the censuses of Ireland from 1901 and 1911, and explore surviving fragments (and substitutes) for previous years, free of charge. All thirty-two counties (for 1901 and 1911) are searchable by all information categories.

Census Research Guide, The National Archives
nationalarchives.gov.uk/records/research-guides/census-returns.htm

This is TNA's general guide to the subject of census returns, which lists what you can learn and some of the official partner subscription websites where you can access the material.

FreeCEN
freecen.org.uk

Part of the freeukgenealogy.org.uk group of websites, FreeCEN provides partial census data from the years 1841, 1851, 1861, 1871, 1881 and 1891. The focus at present is 1891.

The Census, Genuki
genuki.org.uk/big/eng/Census.html

Parts of this Genuki introduction are out of date, but it's a rapid-fire explanation of the various available censuses, with links to both free data and subscription services.

1939 Register Service
hscic.gov.uk/register-service

You can request information about individuals recorded in the 1939 Register for England and Wales via this website.

Belfast Family History
belfastfamilyhistory.com/search.php

Search a database from the 1901 and 1911 Irish census returns, by name or institution.

The 1911 Census
1911census.co.uk

Again includes a free searchable index. You can subscribe via Findmypast or buy credits.

Sheffield Indexers
sheffieldindexers.com/1841Census_Index.html

Complete index to the 1841 census of the region, containing 138,824 records.

Protestation Returns, Parliamentary Archives
www.parliament.uk/business/publications/parliamentary-archives/archives-highlights/familyhistory/sources/protestations/

Described as the closest we have to a census from 1642.

Findmypast
findmypast.co.uk
This site features 1841 to 1911 censuses indexed with images.

The 1901 census
1901censusonline.com
Contains a free searchable index.

UK Census Online
ukcensusonline.com
Has a useful FAQ page.

Ancestry
search.ancestry.co.uk/search/group/ukicen

Census Guide, Society of Genealogists
www.sog.org.uk/learn/help-getting-started-with-genealogy/guide-four

GenesReunited
genesreunited.co.uk

FamilyRelatives
familyrelatives.com

Census Finder
censusfinder.com

1.4 Parish Registers

Parish registers are the primary source for details of births, marriages and deaths prior to the start of the civil registration system. Information recorded within registers does vary, although the system was standardized in 1812. They were maintained by individual churches and the originals usually reside in local archives.

FamilySearch
familysearch.org/learn/wiki/en/England_Church_Records
The LDS Church's International Genealogical Index (IGI), a mass parish-level source, was first published as a computer file in 1973. It now sits alongside vast, ever-expanding indexes, transcriptions and collections of register images, which are sometimes linked to external commercial datasets. This wiki page introduces the subject of church records in England with a useful breakdown of online register images. There are similar guides relating to other parts of the UK.

Parish Registers, Ancestry
ancestry.co.uk/parish
This is the Parish Registers landing page where you can read general background information about parish sources, and latest additions to Ancestry's vast parish

collections, through partner organizations such as the London Metropolitan Archives, and other archives and societies in Dorset, Kent, Lancashire, London, Surrey, Warwickshire and Yorkshire.

FreeREG
freereg.org.uk

The FreeREG database is a volunteer-led drive to provide free online searches of transcribed parish and nonconformist registers. It is constantly growing and updating, so it's definitely worth checking back regularly. If you wish to help, the team are always looking for more volunteers.

ScotlandsPeople
scotlandspeople.gov.uk

From the left-hand column of the homepage you can click Old Parish Registers or Catholic Registers, leading to subdivisions of different life events. It costs £7 to search the registers, which also gives you thirty page-credits (viewing records costs five credits per image).

Essex Ancestors
seax.essexcc.gov.uk/EssexAncestors.aspx

The official Essex Record Office gateway to various sources, including parish registers. You can select parish names and see what material is available and in which format. Where images are available you can register and buy a subscription – from one day (£5) to one year (£85).

Register Copies and Transcripts Guide, Society of Genealogists
sog.org.uk/learn/help-getting-started-with-genealogy/guide-six

This is the excellent SoG guide to parish registers. The SoG itself looks after a huge collection of register copies and transcripts, and you explore material available through Data Online (at sog.ourarchives.info/bin/recordslist.php).

Medway Ancestors
cityark.medway.gov.uk

Medway Archives' online catalogue CityArk, through which you can access the Medway Ancestors database of digitized parish registers, mainly from the Rochester Archdeaconry area – from Dartford and Gravesend in the west, to Rainham in the east.

Parish Records, Findmypast
search.findmypast.co.uk/search-united-kingdom-records-in-birth-marriage-death-and-parish-records

Findmypast BMD and parish register search page. The site is particularly strong on parish material from Cheshire, Devon, Hertfordshire, London, Middlesex, Shropshire, Staffordshire and Yorkshire.

Lincs to the Past
www.lincstothepast.com/help/parish-registers/

This Lincolnshire hub was launched in 2011 and boasts all kinds of fascinating content. This page has a video (or PDF) guide to researching parish registers using the Advanced Search tool.

Bishops' Transcripts Guide, Devon Archives
devon.gov.uk/bishops_transcripts.htm

Devon Archives and Local Studies Service's guide to bishops' transcripts – contemporary copies of parish register entries, which were made and sent annually to the diocesan registry.

Anguline Research Archives
anguline.co.uk

Republishes rare books on CD or via PDF download, including many volumes of UK parish transcriptions from around the turn of the century.

Parish Chest
parishchest.com

Long-established online shop selling a wide range of genealogy products, including parish material, often compiled by family history societies.

Cornwall Online Parish Clerks
cornwall-opc.org

Cornwall was the birthplace of the OPC scheme, and here you can access a free index/transcription database of parish registers.

Federation of Family History Societies
ffhs.org.uk

Find member websites for local parish transcriptions and find out about collaborative nationwide projects such as the National Burial Index.

FamilyRelatives
familyrelatives.com

To see what parish material is available from this commercial site, select Parish Registers from the Search drop-down menu.

S&N Genealogy
genealogysupplies.com

Genealogical shop and the team behind TheGenealogist. Offers lots of transcribed parish registers on CD and in other formats.

London Registers
www.parishregister.com

Offers transcribed parish data covering London, particularly the Docklands.

TheGenealogist, Parish Records
thegenealogist.co.uk/parish_records/
Datasets include the noted Phillimore transcripts of marriages.

Online Parish Clerks, UK BMD
ukbmd.org.uk/online_parish_clerk
Useful links page that lists Online Parish Clerk websites from counties across England.

GENFair
GENFair.co.uk
Online genealogical shop with thousands of parish records in various formats.

Dorset Online Parish Clerks
opcdorset.org
At the time of writing, this site boasted more than 1.6 million records.

BMD Registers
bmdregisters.co.uk
Commercial hub for nonconformist registers.

Devon Online Parish Clerks
genuki.cs.ncl.ac.uk/DEV/OPCproject.html

Essex Online Parish Clerks
essex-opc.org.uk

Kent Online Parish Clerks
kent-opc.org

Hampshire Online Parish Clerks
knightroots.co.uk

Lancashire Online Parish Clerks
lan-opc.org.uk

Leicestershire Genealogical Resources
rootsweb.ancestry.com/~engleiopc/

Somerset Online Parish Clerks
wsom-opc.org.uk

Sussex Online Parish Clerks
sussex-opc.org

Warwickshire Online Parish Clerks
hunimex.com/warwick/opc/opc.html

Wiltshire Online Parish Clerks
wiltshire-opc.org.uk

Cheshire Parish Register Project
cgi.csc.liv.ac.uk/~cprdb/

Sheffield Indexers, Parish Registers
sheffieldindexers.com/ParishBaptismIndex.html

Cumberland and Westmorland Parish Registers
cumberlandarchives.co.uk

Registers, UK Genealogy Archives
ukga.org/Registers/

See also: 1.2 GRO Indexes, 2.1 Burial Records and Monumental Inscriptions, 2.2 Probate and Wills, 2.20 Nonconformist, 3.13 War Graves, 5.1 Resources by Region

Section 2

DIGGING DEEPER

2.1 Burial Records and Monumental Inscriptions (MIs)

A gravestone can provide information not found in written records – it may list immediate family, give biographical details and allow you to make judgements about status. The genealogical society for an area will often have produced MI transcriptions in various formats. There's no central registry of burial and/or cremation data, but there are major commercial players who specialize in MIs and burial records. Remember too that volunteer groups and some councils compile and maintain cemetery databases.

Gravestone Photos
gravestonephotos.com

A growing photographic resource launched in 1998, which aims to photograph and index monuments across the globe (coverage is dominated by England and Scotland). The data includes all legible personal information from each gravestone and the site claims that an average of twelve new cemeteries are added each week. It currently focuses on monuments for people born before 1901.

Deceased Online
deceasedonline.com

Leading commercial specialists, providing data from graveyards and municipal cemeteries across the UK. You can search – by country, region, county, burial authority or crematorium – free of charge, but you will need to register and pay in order to see digital scans of cremation/burial registers, photographs of graves and memorials, plus cemetery maps.

Commonwealth War Graves Commission
www.cwgc.org/find-a-cemetery.aspx

This address takes you to the CWGC's Find a Cemetery page, where you can search information about 23,000 cemeteries and memorials across the globe. These lead to maps, plans and pictures, plus you have the ability to search names preserved in a particular location.

Discovereverafter
discovereverafter.com

Hosts a growing collection of burial data for genealogists, which is mainly from Ireland. The team has also launched cloud platform PlotBox, an administrative tool designed for cemeteries and crematoria, which should see lots more burial records pouring onto Discovereverafter.

Interment
interment.net

Free library of Cemetery Records Online, drawn from cemeteries and graveyards across the globe. There's a great deal of UK material but coverage is patchy – currently seventeen datasets for Cleveland alone, one single record for all of East Sussex.

National Burial Index
ffhs.org.uk/burials/nbi-overview.php

Federation of FHS overview of the ongoing National Burial Index project. The third edition contains over 18.4 million entries, harvested from some 9,100 locations in 50 counties and is currently available via Findmypast.

National Burial Index, Findmypast
findmypast.co.uk

Hosts the aforementioned National Burial Index plus lots of MI data available through society partnerships. Use the A–Z list of record sets to find and search individual collections. For more MI news go to: blog.findmypast.co.uk/tag/monumental-inscriptions/.

Death, Burial, Cemetery and Obituary, Ancestry
search.ancestry.co.uk/search/category.aspx?cat=125

Here you can view sample images and details of all Ancestry's death, burial, cemetery and obituary collections. The right-hand column allows you to filter by location and date.

Burial Inscriptions
burial-inscriptions.co.uk

Guy Etchells is a genealogical mover and shaker with several projects on the go, including online shop anguline.co.uk. This is his burial hub, which links to vast amounts of online burial/MI data.

Sheffield Indexers
sheffieldindexers.com/BurialIndex.html

Sheffield Indexers provides transcriptions of all sorts of genealogical records and this page lists the current graveyards and cemeteries contained within the burial database.

Death and Burial, GenesReunited

genesreunited.co.uk/articles/world-records/full-list-of-united-kingdom-records/births-marriages-and-deaths/deaths-and-burials

This page lists all the Death and Burial datasets available here – such as 170,855 MI records from the county of Essex.

Manchester Burial Records

www.burialrecords.manchester.gov.uk

Manchester City Council site that allows you to search a database of burial and cremation records from six municipal cemeteries.

Wrexham Cemetery Burials

wrexham.gov.uk/english/community/genealogy/cemeteries_search/Cemeteries IndexSearchForm.cfm

Free database of burials at the authority's main Wrexham Cemetery going back to 1876 (when the cemetery opened).

Belfast Burials

belfastcity.gov.uk/community/burialrecords/burialrecords.aspx

Search 360,000 Belfast burial records, from three cemeteries, dating back to 1869. You can buy images of burial records for £1.50 each.

GraveMatters

gravematters.org.uk

Tips and advice about transcribing MIs.

Haverhill Cemetery Burial Records

haverhill-uk.com/pages/burial-records-137.htm

Kingston upon Thames Burial Records

kingston.gov.uk/info/200136/funerals_cremations_and_cemeteries/342/search_our_burial_records

World Burial Index

worldburialindex.com

London Burial Grounds

londonburials.co.uk

Highland Memorial Inscriptions

sites.google.com/site/highlandmemorialinscriptions/home

See also: 1.2 GRO Indexes, 1.4 Parish Registers, 2.2 Probate and Wills, 2.7 Coroners' Inquests, 3.13 War Graves, 5.1 Resources by Region

2.2 Probate and Wills

Wills and probate documents can give you all kinds of details about a person's life, wealth and relationships. But they can also be confusing, hard to find, fragmentary and written in Latin. There's a natural assumption that only the more well-to-do left wills, but this is not always the case. Plus there's a chance you may find references to your ancestor in other people's wills.

Wills and Probate, The National Archives

nationalarchives.gov.uk/records/wills-and-probate.htm

The National Archives has several research guides that investigate both the great potential and difficulty of using probate documents. This particular Our Online Records page details available datasets such as Wills 1384–1858 (from the Prerogative Court of Canterbury), Wills of RN and Royal Marines Personnel (1786–1882), County Court Death Duty Registers and Famous Wills (1552–1854).

North East Inheritance Database

familyrecords.dur.ac.uk/nei/data/intro.php

Part of the Durham University Library special collections site, this is a database of pre-1858 probate records (wills and related documents) covering Northumberland and County Durham. Digital images of the original probate records (including wills and inventories, 1650–1857; copies of wills, 1527–1858; and executors' and administration bonds, 1702–1858) are now available through FamilySearch.

National Wills Index, Findmypast

findmypast.co.uk/search/probate-and-wills

Origins Network launched a dedicated probate hub, the nationalwillsindex.com, which is the largest resource for pre-1858 English probate material online, containing indexes, abstracts and source documents. As with the rest of Origins it is now part of DC Thomson Family History, so the data is available via Findmypast.

Probate Search, GOV.uk

probatesearch.service.gov.uk/#wills

Official government database that allows you to search an archive of 41 million wills dating back to 1858. A name and year of death are required to find wills; these should be ready for download within ten days of ordering – which costs £10. It also includes wills of those who died while serving in the British armed forces between 1850 and 1986.

National Library of Wales

cat.llgc.org.uk/probate

Search wills proved in the Welsh ecclesiastical courts prior to the introduction of civil probate in 1858. You can either search the entire index, or narrow it down to individual probate collections. Any hits link through to free digital images of the original documents.

ScotlandsPeople
scotlandspeople.gov.uk

Trawl the free index to over 611,000 entries for Scottish wills and testaments dating from 1513 to 1901 (listing surname, forename, title, occupation and place of residence), plus the more recently released database of Soldiers' Wills.

Wiltshire Wills
history.wiltshire.gov.uk/heritage/

Catalogue to wills and probate records of the diocese of Salisbury (1540–1858), covering Wiltshire, Berkshire and parts of Dorset and Devon. Search by name, place, occupation and date. You can pay to view digital images of some documents.

Public Record Office of Northern Ireland
www.proni.gov.uk/index/search_the_archives.htm

This page has details of all PRONI's online collections, including Will Calendars – a free index of wills from the District Probate Registries of Armagh, Belfast and Londonderry (1858–1943). There are digitized images up to 1900.

England Probate Records, FamilySearch
familysearch.org/learn/wiki/en/England_Probate_Records

FamilySearch wiki on probate material in England, which links to articles on probate material elsewhere, plus the site's own collections – such as images of Kent Wills and Probate (1440–1881).

Wills and Probate, Ancestry
search.ancestry.co.uk/search/

To explore the vast amount of probate material available through Ancestry, start at this search page, click Search and choose Wills and Probate from the drop-down menu; currently there are fifty-eight UK collections.

Soldiers' and Airmen's wills, National Records of Scotland,
nrscotland.gov.uk/research/guides/soldiers-and-airmens-wills

Guide to the searchable wills of soldiers and airmen between 1857–1964 (now available via ScotlandsPeople).

Soldiers' Wills, National Archives of Ireland
soldierswills.nationalarchives.ie

The National Archives of Ireland's collection of wills of Irish soldiers who died while serving in the British army during the Great War. Also, at willcalendars.nationalarchives.ie/search/cwa/home.jsp, you can search Calendars of Wills and Administrations (1858–1922).

Essex Wills

seax.essexcc.gov.uk

Search and access images of Essex wills (*c*.1400–1720) held at Essex Record Office, with more on the way.

Gloucestershire Wills

ww3.gloucestershire.gov.uk/genealogy/Search.aspx

The county archives' Genealogical Search page includes inventories plus wills between 1541 and 1858.

Probate Records Guide, Society of Genealogists

sog.org.uk/learn/help-getting-started-with-genealogy/guide-five

The SoG research guide introducing probate records as sources for family history.

The Gazette

www.thegazette.co.uk/wills-and-probate

Wills and probate notices printed in the London, Edinburgh and Belfast Gazettes.

Probate Guide, TheGenealogist

thegenealogist.co.uk/researchguide/?cid=1&p=108t

Research guide which lists the numerous datasets available here.

Recent Indexes to Probate Records

community.dur.ac.uk/a.r.millard/genealogy/probate.php

A list of probate indexes, many of which are available online.

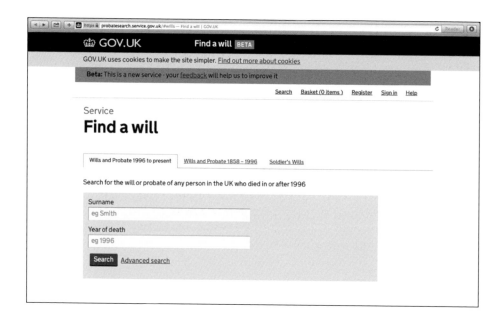

Bristol Record Office
archive.today/wZyL
Web archive page of indexes to Bristol-proved wills (1781–1858).

Cheshire Wills
archivedatabases.cheshire.gov.uk/RecordOfficeWillEPayments/search.aspx
Cheshire Archives and Local Studies' wills database.

See also: 1.2 GRO Indexes, 1.4 Parish Registers, 2.1 Burial Records and Monumental Inscriptions, 2.6 Court Records, 2.24 Estate Records, 2.25 Seventeenth- and Eighteenth-Century Sources, 5.4 House History, 5.5 Medieval Ancestors, 5.7 Nobility and Gentry

2.3 Taxation

Taxation records can tell you a lot about your forebear's assets, earnings and general status. Indeed if you're lucky enough to be able to trace your lineage back to before parish registers began in the sixteenth century, then it is taxation records that offer the best hope for tracing individuals.

Hearth Tax Online
hearthtax.org.uk
Between 1662 and 1689 the hearth tax was levied on each householder according to the number of hearths in his or her dwelling. The results represent a kind of census, recording the head-of-household of each property as well as giving you an idea of wealth. The site covers many counties and also includes maps and background articles.

Taxation, The National Archives
apps.nationalarchives.gov.uk/e179/
This page hosts the E 179 database of 'particulars of account and other records relating to lay and clerical taxation'. You can search the database by place, grant of taxation, date or type of document. There are related research guides to taxation, including taxation prior to 1689, plus the Domesday Book (nationalarchives.gov.uk/domesday/).

West Yorkshire Tithe Maps Project
tracksintime.wyjs.org.uk
Tithe apportionment maps were drawn up for many parishes across England and Wales, with corresponding schedule books describing land use, rentable value, and names of owners/occupiers. Here you can explore the maps, compare them with modern maps, and search apportionment data for individuals. (See 2.23 Maps for more information on tithes.)

Griffith's Valuation

askaboutireland.ie/griffith-valuation/index.xml

Home to the famous property tax survey of Ireland, which saw the detailed valuation of every taxable piece of agricultural or built property, and was published county by county between the years 1847 and 1864. The valuation books recorded the names of occupiers and landowners, and the amount and value of the property held.

Wills, Probate and Tax, Ancestry

ancestry.co.uk/cs/uk/probate

Ancestry's Wills, Probate and Tax landing page, from where you can learn about collections such as London Land Tax Records (1692–1932), produced in partnership with London Metropolitan Archives, and other regional collections such as Birmingham Rate Books (1831–1913).

Rate Books, Findmypast

findmypast.co.uk/articles/world-records/search-all-uk-records/census-land-and-survey—records/rate-books

Introduction to rate books, which list the owners/occupiers of properties on which rates were paid. Here you can search rate-book collections from Plymouth and West Devon (1598–1933), Westminster (1634–1900), Manchester (1706–1900) and Southwark (1821 and 1831).

ScotlandsPlaces

scotlandsplaces.gov.uk

Hosts data relating to servant tax rolls, the farm horse tax, inhabited house tax rolls (1778–98), the clock and watch tax, land tax and more. Some material is free, some via subscription. In late 2014 it was bolstered by poll tax records from the 1690s.

Valuation Rolls, ScotlandsPeople

scotlandspeople.gov.uk/content/help/index.aspx?r=554&2080

Following an Act of 1854 there were annual valuation rolls listing every house or piece of ground in Scotland, along with the names/designations of proprietor, tenant and occupier.

Building History

buildinghistory.org/taxation.shtml

Useful linked guide to taxation relating to property, explaining the background of each tax and where records are likely to be found.

Hair Powder Tax, Wikipedia

en.wikipedia.org/wiki/Duty_on_Hair_Powder_Act_1795

A Wikipedia entry that covers systems of UK taxation both well-known and obscure. This page details the eighteenth-century Duty on Hair Powder Act.

Scottish Taxation, National Records of Scotland

nrscotland.gov.uk/research/guides/taxation-records

Guide to taxation records by National Records of Scotland, with links to various datasets that are available online.

HM Waterguard

hm-waterguard.org.uk/History.htm

Explores the history, structure, manpower and work of the Preventive Service of HM Customs and Excise.

Glasgow Valuation Rolls

theglasgowstory.com/valsearch.php

Explore the Glasgow Valuation Rolls for 1913–14.

Taxatio Database

hrionline.ac.uk/taxatio/

Database of ecclesiastical taxation assessment of 1291–2.

See also: 2.23 Maps, 2.25 Seventeenth- and Eighteenth-Century Sources, 4.16 Coastguard and Customs, 5.5 Medieval Ancestors, 5.7 Nobility and Gentry

2.4 Election Records

Election records can be useful for confirming basic information about your ancestors. Early poll books – which should give you names, addresses, occupations and how a person voted – pre-date census records; electoral registers, first introduced in 1832, contain the details of everyone who qualified to vote and often survive in local history collections.

Chartist Ancestors

chartists.net

Fascinating website that draws on national and local newspaper accounts, court records, contemporary books, later histories and other sources to create a detailed overview of the great Chartist movement of the Victorian period. The site has lots of lists and databases of individuals involved, plus advice on how and where you can begin your own research.

Electoral Registers, Findmypast

findmypast.co.uk/articles/world-records/search-all-uk-records/census-land-and-survey—records/electoral-rolls

Landing page for Findmypast's census, land and survey records, which includes the likes of Cheshire electoral registers (1842–1900). Since taking over origins.net, the site also boasts Somerset electoral registers, which cover the years 1832 to 1914 and feature more than 2 million entries.

Electoral Registers, British Library

bl.uk/reshelp/findhelprestype/offpubs/electreg/electoral.html

Guide to the British Library's national collection of electoral registers from 1832 to the present day (although the collection is patchy prior to the Second World War). You can also download the PDF *Parliamentary Constituencies and their Registers Since 1832* by Richard Cheffins.

Electoral Registers, FamilySearch

familysearch.org/search/collection/2228170

Hosts unindexed collections of registers from Norfolk (1844–1952), Cheshire (1842–1900), West Glamorgan (1839–1925) and Kent (1570–1907). This particular address takes you to London registers (1847–1913) filmed at the London Metropolitan Archives.

Poll Books, TheGenealogist

thegenealogist.co.uk/researchguide/?cid=1&p=141

This page includes a research guide to poll books and details of those available to TheGenealogist subscribers. There's also a case study of the father of the Brontë sisters, recorded in the 1835 poll book for West Riding, Yorkshire.

Parliamentary Archives

www.parliament.uk/about/living-heritage/transformingsociety/electionsvoting/

Living Heritage draws from all sorts of material kept in the Parliamentary Archives to create themed, illustrated galleries relating to the Chartist and Suffragette movements.

Ancestry, Census and Electoral Rolls

search.ancestry.co.uk/search/db.aspx?dbid=2410

Has the UK Poll Books and Electoral Registers (1538–1893) collection. Ancestry also has election material from Nottinghamshire, Dorset, Warwickshire, Birmingham and elsewhere.

Valuation and Voters' Rolls, National Library of Scotland

www.nls.uk/family-history/voters-rolls

Page describing the NLS holdings, which include almost all electoral registers from 1946.

Dublin Electoral Lists

dublinheritage.ie/burgesses/index.php

Free access to Dublin electoral registers for the years 1908 to 1912, and 1915 (with more to follow).

Electoral Registers

electoralregisters.org.uk

Information page with links to online sources of electoral registers.

County Durham Registers, Archive.org
archive.org/stream/registervotersf00coungoog#page/n12/mode/2up

Chartist Movement, BBC History
bbc.co.uk/history/british/victorians/chartist_01.shtml

2.5 Crime and Punishment

Court records are covered in more detail in the next chapter, so here the focus is on other kinds of records and digital resources relating to crime and punishment. These include sites that offer research advice, social histories, and avenues to records relating to prisoners and prisons, and other forms of punishment.

Crimes and Prisoners, The National Archives
nationalarchives.gov.uk/records/looking-for-person/criminal-trial-or-conviction.htm

TNA guide to its criminal or convict holdings. There are also guides focusing specifically on prisoners, civil litigants, criminal transports and bankrupts/debtors. You can explore prisoner photograph albums from Wandsworth Prison (1872–3) which include prisoners' physical descriptions, birth details, crimes committed, sentences, places of conviction and residences after release (nationalarchives. gov.uk/records/victorian-prisoners-photographs.htm).

Criminal Records, Ancestry
ancestry.co.uk/cs/uk/criminal

Details regional and national collections that include West Yorkshire criminal records (1779–1914), comprising data from three reform schools. There's also the Bedfordshire Gaol Index (1770–1882), Birmingham prisoners (1880–1913), the UK-wide Criminal Registers (1791–1892), Prison Hulk Registers (1802–49) Australian Transportation (1787–1868). In addition, there's a collection of Debtors' Prison Registers (1734–1862).

Crime, Prisons and Punishment, Findmypast
search.findmypast.co.uk/search-world-records/crime-prisons-and-punishment

More than 515,000 records of criminals who passed through the justice system in England and Wales between 1770 and 1934, produced in partnership with The National Archives. Material comprises the Home Office calendar of prisoners, which includes 301,359 people for the period 1869 to 1929.

Convict Transportation Registers Database
www.slq.qld.gov.au/resources/family-history/convicts

Information on more than 123,000 of the 160,000 convicts transported to Australia between 1787 and 1867, which is included in the Convict Transportation Registers Series (HO 11) held at The National Archives. For more information, or to find similar online sources, scroll down to Related Websites.

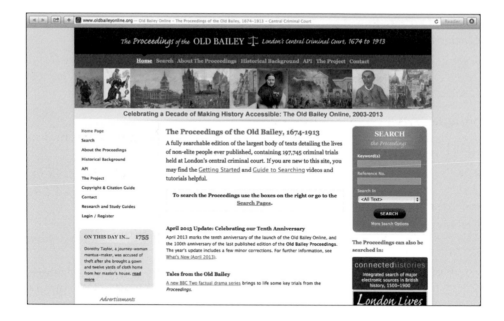

Proceedings of the Old Bailey
www.oldbaileyonline.org

Endlessly fascinating and completely free database of 197,745 criminal trials held at London's Central Criminal Court from 1674 up to 1913. You can search by various fields including punishment, filtering results by imprisonment, hard labour, house of correction, Newgate or penal servitude.

Lancaster Castle
lancastercastle.com/Archives

Includes information about the castle's famous history as a place of punishment, including the infamous case of the Lancashire witches. There's also a complete convict database, which lists inmates who were tried and sentenced at Lancaster Assizes.

Discovery
discovery.nationalarchives.gov.uk

Many local record offices will have guides to their relevant holdings online, or catalogued prison collections. Catalogues from UK-wide archives, formally available through A2A, have now been incorporated into TNA's Discovery.

London Lives
londonlives.org

Explores crime in the metropolis between 1690 and 1800. Part of the Connected Histories family (connectedhistories.org). For more information on individual prisons, go to londonlives.org/static/Prisons.jsp.

Blacksheep Ancestors
blacksheepancestors.com/uk/prisons.shtml

Despite a testing layout and out-of-date links, there is useful material to be found here, including various indexes drawn from the census, such as the 1901 index to Canterbury Prison and an 1881 equivalent for Brixton Prison.

Victorian Prisoners Aylesbury Gaol
www.buckscc.gov.uk/leisure-and-culture/centre-for-buckinghamshire-studies/online-resources/victorian-prisoners/

The Centre for Buckinghamshire Studies site has a database of prisoners from Aylesbury Gaol in the 1870s, drawn from information contained within gaol receiving books.

Plymouth Prisoners, Plymouth and West Devon Record Office
plymouth.gov.uk/cemeterymortuaryworkhouse

Another example of local holdings, Plymouth Archives has indexed registers to prisoners between 1867 and 1930, plus a register of prison officers from the late nineteenth century to 1926.

Manchester Research
www.manchester-family-history-research.co.uk/new_page_17.htm

Manchester researcher Gerard Lodge's data-rich website includes lots of material relating to Belle Vue Prison, New Bailey Prison, Strangeways and Millbank.

Bath Prisoners
batharchives.co.uk/bath-ancestors

The Bath Record Office's Bath Ancestors Database includes prisoner portrait books from the 1890s, taken from the Bath City Police archives.

1901 Census Institution Search
1901censusonline.com/search.asp?wci=institution_search

Reveals who was living in prisons, workhouses and other institutions on census night.

Gazettes Online
www.thegazette.co.uk

Search official notices published in the Gazettes, including notices of bankruptcies.

Crime and Criminals, National Records of Scotland
nrscotland.gov.uk/research/research-guides/court-and-legal-records

Illustrated NRS guide to sources for researching crime in Scotland.

Crime and Punishment Database, National Library of Wales
www.llgc.org.uk/sesiwn_fawr/index_s.htm

Search gaol files of the Court of Great Sessions in Wales (1730–1830).

Criminal Records, Society of Genealogists
www.sog.org.uk/learn/help-getting-started-with-genealogy/guide-7-criminal-records
Useful SoG guide to the subject of criminal records.

Crime and Punishment, Devon County Council
devon.gov.uk/crime
Example of a regional guide to relevant sources.

POA History in Prisons
poauk.org.uk/index.php?poa-history-in-prisons
The history of the trade union for prison workers.

Scottish Prison Service
sps.gov.uk/Prisons/prisons.aspx
Lists Scottish prisons, each with a brief history.

Inveraray Jail
www.inverarayjail.co.uk/our-story/prisoner-records/
Has records for over 4,000 former prisoners.

Debtors, Victorian Crime and Punishment
vcp.e2bn.org/justice/page11365-debtors.html

See also: 1.3 The Census, 2.6 Court Records, 2.8 Poor Law and Workhouses, 4.2 Police

2.6 Court Records

When delving into court material it is important to find out in which court a trial was heard: police or magistrates' court, quarter sessions or assizes, or church court. Many local repositories will have online guides or catalogues to their court collections, and some are available through commercial websites. There's also the large-scale criminal records partnership between TNA and Findmypast.

The National Archives, Assizes
nationalarchives.gov.uk/records/research-guides/assizes-criminal-1559-1971.htm
TNA holds many records of criminal trials, although they are scattered with no central name index. There are several different TNA guides which touch on the subject, exploring what is held where and linking to online material available through commercial partners. Generally TNA has records of the assizes, while records of quarter sessions/petty sessions held at magistrates' courts will be at local archives.

Criminal Registers, Ancestry
search.ancestry.co.uk/search/db.aspx?dbid=1590
Ancestry's criminal registers for England and Wales between 1791 and 1892 (TNA ref HO 26 and HO 27). The registers provide dates and locations of the court

hearings which can point you towards other sources such as local newspapers. Down the right side of the screen you can browse other regional and national collections.

The Cause Papers Database, Diocese of York

hrionline.ac.uk/causepapers/

Searchable catalogue of more than 14,000 cause papers relating to cases heard between 1300 and 1858 in the church courts of the diocese of York. The courts had jurisdiction over cases involving issues of matrimony, defamation, tithe, probate and church rights.

Crime and Punishment Database, National Library of Wales

www.llgc.org.uk/sesiwn_fawr/index_s.htm

Crimes, criminals and punishments included in the gaol files of the Court of Great Sessions in Wales from 1730 until its abolition in 1830. The court could try all types of crimes, from petty thefts to high treason.

London Court Records

londonlives.org

Searchable edition of 240,000 manuscripts from 8 archives, which boasts 3.35 million names. The Browse page lists some of the court records such as those taken from the City of London, Middlesex, and Westminster sessions.

Crime, Prisons and Punishment, Findmypast

search.findmypast.co.uk/search-world-records/crime-prisons-and-punishment

The result of a TNA partnership, this collection has 515,000 records ranging from petitions for clemency to entry books, judges' reports, prison registers, transfer papers and gaolers' reports.

Old Bailey Online

www.oldbaileyonline.org

Search Old Bailey trials (1674–1913) by name, alias and keyword, and narrow the results by time period, type of offence, verdict or punishment.

Court and Legal Records, National Records of Scotland

nrscotland.gov.uk/research/research-guides/court-and-legal-records

Handy NRS guide with information on each category of court material. From the A–Z list you can also find the guides to Court of Session Records, and Crime and Criminals.

York Assizes

yorkfamilyhistory.org.uk/assizes.htm

Index to records – held in York Reference Library – of prisoners brought to trial at York Assizes in the period 1785–1851, produced by the City of York and District FHS.

BBC History, Crime

bbc.co.uk/history/familyhistory/next_steps/adv_10_crime_01.shtml

Useful article from Dr Nick Barratt, introducing the kind of information recorded at quarter sessions and assizes.

Scottish Archive Network, Virtual Vault

scan.org.uk/researchrtools/courtrecords.htm

See also: 2.5 Crime and Punishment, 2.7 Coroners' Inquests, 2.8 Poor Law and Workhouses

2.7 Coroners' Inquests

If your ancestor died in unexplained circumstances there may have been a coroner's inquest, often conducted at a local alehouse, workhouse or the actual building where the death occurred. Up to 1752, coroners handed records to assize judges; these records were eventually transferred to The National Archives. Inquests held from 1860 onwards were filed through the quarter sessions, meaning those that survive will usually be at local archives.

Coroners' Inquests into Suspicious Deaths, LondonLives

londonlives.org/static/IC.jsp

Excellent introduction to the subject, where you can explore, free of charge, digital images and transcriptions of around 5,000 inquests from the City of London, and Middlesex and Westminster.

British Newspaper Archive

britishnewspaperarchive.co.uk

Newspaper reports will often represent the only surviving account of an inquest, and here you can search newspapers by title, area and date range, and of course search by name or keyword.

Fatal Accident Inquiries, The National Archives of Scotland

www.nas.gov.uk/guides/FAI.asp

Fatal accident inquiries were processed through the sheriff courts, and most are listed in the NAS online catalogue. There's also a National Records of Scotland guide to Sheriff Court Records (nrscotland.gov.uk/research/guides/sheriff-court-records).

Salisbury Inquests

salisburyinquests.wordpress.com

Contains transcribed press reports of coroners' inquests for the period between 1868 and 1920, covering Salisbury and South Wiltshire. You can search by name or keyword, or browse cases by year.

Coroners' Inquests, Public Records Office of Northern Ireland

www.proni.gov.uk/index/search_the_archives/proninames/coroners__inquest_
papers-_whats_available.htm

PRONI looks after coroners' records from 1872 to 1997, and 6,206 files/papers
relating to inquests are now referenced via the online Name Search.

Hertfordshire Coroners' Inquests

hertsdirect.org/services/leisculture/heritage1/hals/famhist/coroner/

Details of material held at Hertfordshire Archives and Local Studies. There's also
an index to fatalities between 1827 and 1933.

Devon Inquests

devon.gov.uk/index/councildemocracy/record_office/information_about_devon
_heritage_services/guide_sources/coroners__records_in_devon.htm

Devon Heritage Centre's guide to its inquest holdings, including a list of names
from Exeter reports going back to 1702.

Sussex Record Society

sussexrecordsociety.org

Among the society's free-to-view online books is the title: *Notes of Post Mortem
Inquisitions Taken in Sussex* (which covers the dates between 1485 and 1649).

Coroners' Inquests, TNA Podcast

media.nationalarchives.gov.uk/index.php/coroners-inquests/

Podcast lecture given by TNA's Dr Kathy Chater.

Medieval Coroner

britannia.com/history/articles/coroner1.html

History of the origins and development of the coroner system.

Coroners' Inquests Guide, The National Archives

nationalarchives.gov.uk/records/looking-for-person/coroners-inquests.htm

Death by Misadventure: Coroners' Inquests 1700–1850

stamfordhistory.org.uk/publications/death-misadventure-coroners-inquests-
1700-1850-part-1

Coroner Inquest Records, GenGuide

genguide.co.uk/source/Coroner-Inquest-Records-Crime-amp-Courts/99/

New South Wales, Australia, Coroners' Inquests (1796–1942), Ancestry

search.ancestry.co.uk/search/db.aspx?dbid=1785

See also: 2.5 Crime and Punishment, 2.6 Court Records

2.8 Poor Law and Workhouses

If an individual fell on hard times there were various institutions that might have dealt with the case. Before 1834, care for the destitute rested largely on the parish. Later it was administered by Poor Law Unions run by an elected board of guardians. Most Poor Law material is held locally, although wider Poor Law Commission records are at The National Archives.

The Workhouse
workhouses.org.uk

Wonderful encyclopaedic guide to the workhouse system from expert Peter Higginbotham, with histories and images of individual workhouses, all searchable by Poor Law location. It's useful in a practical sense for finding out where workhouse records are held, but there's also so much here for the casual browser – fascinating articles, first-hand accounts, examples of all kinds of original documents, photographs and plans, and more.

Poor Law Unions' Gazette, British Newspaper Archive
britishnewspaperarchive.co.uk

From the home page select the newspaper title drop-down menu, scroll down and you'll find the Poor Law Unions' Gazette (1857–65). As Peter Higginbotham notes in workhouses.org: 'Its contents consisted entirely of detailed "wanted" descriptions of men who had deserted their families and left the union to take care of them.'

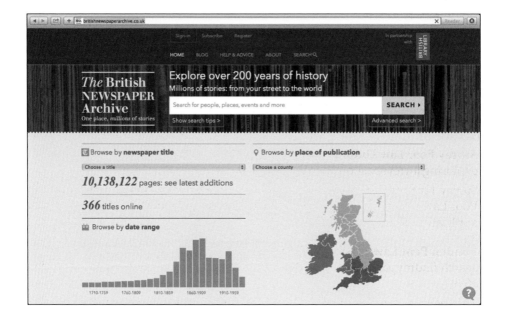

Settlement Certificates and Removal Orders, GenGuide

genguide.co.uk/source/settlement-certificatesexaminations-and-removal-orders-parish-amp-poor-law/173/

Guide to parish-level sources generated from Settlement Certificates/ Examinations and Removal Orders. There are also pages dedicated to Apprenticeship Indentures, Bastardy Bonds, Overseers of the Poor Accounts and Workhouse Records.

England and Wales Poor Law Wiki, FamilySearch

familysearch.org/learn/wiki/en/England_and_Wales_Poor_Law_Records_1834 -1948

The best route to FamilySearch's Poor Law material is through this wiki page, which also serves as an excellent introduction to the subject, before linking to Poor Law collections from Norfolk, Kent and Cheshire.

Poor Laws Guide, The National Archives

nationalarchives.gov.uk/records/research-guides/poor-laws.htm

There are allied guides to workhouse records as well. You can also search the Discovery catalogue (discovery.nationalarchives.gov.uk/SearchUI/) and download (for a fee) records from more than twenty Poor Law Unions from 1834.

Childrenshomes

childrenshomes.org.uk

Sister site to workhouses.org, which gives details of orphanages, homes for those in poverty or with special needs, reformatories, industrial and approved schools, training ships and more.

Poor Law, Ancestry

search.ancestry.co.uk/search/db.aspx?dbid=1557

London Poor Law and Board of Guardian Records (1430–1930), produced in partnership with the London Metropolitan Archives, plus collections from Warwickshire, Dorset and Norfolk. They also have collections recording men and women who were put into debtors' prisons.

Surrey Poor Law Unions

exploringsurreyspast.org.uk/indexes/

Surrey History Centre site with various online indexes including the Chertsey Poor Law Union admission and discharge books and Godstone Poor Law Union application and report books.

London Poor Law Abstracts, Findmypast

search.findmypast.co.uk/world-records/search-london-poor-law-records-1581-1899

This section includes London Poor Law Abstracts, formerly available through origins.net, plus Poor Law/workhouse material from Lincolnshire, Cheshire, Derbyshire and Manchester.

Paupers in Workhouses 1861
genuki.org.uk/big/eng/Paupers/
Genuki-hosted 10 per cent sample of adult paupers in England and Wales, as originally recorded in a House of Commons Parliamentary Paper.

Manchester Family History Research
manchester-family-history-research.co.uk
Home to all kinds of useful information for Manchester researchers, including sections dedicated to various industrial schools, plus Poor Law and workhouse records.

Waifs and Strays' Society
hiddenlives.org.uk
In late Victorian and early twentieth-century Britain, this charitable society cared for 22,500 children. The site includes lists and histories of the homes, plus sample case files.

Charles Booth Online Archive
booth.lse.ac.uk
View images of the original Stepney Union casebooks, drawn from Booth's famous survey of life and labour in London, dating from 1886 to 1903.

West Sussex Poor Law Database
sussexrecordsociety.org
Sussex Record Society website hosts this index to individuals documented in the Poor Law records – listing date, reference, name, parish and type of record.

Dundee Poorhouse Records
fdca.org.uk/Dundee_Poorhouses.html
Friends of Dundee City Archives' guide and online index to poor registers.

Workhouse Museum, Ripon
ripon.co.uk/museums/

Manchester Poor Law and Workhouse Records
manchester.gov.uk/info/448/archives_and_local_history/3812/poor_law_and_workhouse_records

London Lives: Crime, Poverty and Social Policy in the Metropolis
londonlives.org

The Union Workhouse
www.judandk.force9.co.uk/workhouse.html

Care of the Poor, Powys Digital History Project
history.powys.org.uk/history/common/poormenu.html

Ragged School Museum
raggedschoolmuseum.org.uk

Foundling Museum
foundlingmuseum.org.uk

See also: 2.6 Court Records, 4.19 Other Occupations and Apprentices

2.9 Schools and Universities

School records can not only tell you about your ancestor's education, but also offer a window to the wider community. School log books in particular often have references to local celebrations, bouts of sickness, harvests, civic celebrations and national events. Before the Findmypast/multi-archive digitization project, the majority were only available at local archives.

National School Admission Registers 1870–1914, Findmypast
blog.findmypast.co.uk/2014/2-5-million-school-records-published/

In September 2014, Findmypast published the first tranche of its National School Admission Registers 1870 to 1914 collection. The project was coordinated by The National Archives, and the Archives and Records Association (archives.org.uk), and launched with 2.5 million school records drawn from archives across England and Wales, including handwritten registers, log books and attendance records. This page tells you more about the project, with a link to the records themselves. Admission registers were usually kept from around 1870, and give the name of the child, date of birth, date of admission to the school, plus father's name, address and sometimes occupation.

Hidden Lives
hiddenlives.org.uk

Explores the lives and schooling of children who were in the care of the Children's Society (formerly the Waifs and Strays' Society) from 1881. There's a complete list of the homes, often with photographs, drawings and histories, plus you can browse various Children's Society journals.

Radley College Archives
radleyarchives.co.uk

Digital archive from this Oxfordshire school, featuring registers, staff records, photographs, newsletters and manuscript collections. There are also photograph albums showing alumni who served and lost their lives in both world wars.

Scottish Archive Network
scan.org.uk/researchrtools/schoollogbook.htm

You can search for school material through this single catalogue to records in fifty-two Scottish archives. This particular address takes you to high-quality digital images from Aberdeenshire Archives' Pitsligo School log book, between 1874 and 1912.

London School Admissions and Discharges, 1840–1911, Ancestry

search.ancestry.co.uk/search/db.aspx?dbid=1938

Digitized from the London Metropolitan Archives' school collections, this dataset contains more than a million students from 843 different schools.

Manchester High School for Girls Archive

www.mhsgarchive.org

Online archive where you can explore letters, governors' minutes, newspaper cuttings, programmes, school magazines and reports.

Sheffield Indexers

sheffieldindexers.com/SchoolsIndex.html

Page listing the transcribed school admission registers available free of charge through this website.

Bristol Schools

bristolinformation.co.uk/schools/

Click List All Schools on the left-hand menu to explore a list of Bristol schools, gathered from a variety of sources dating back to the sixteenth century.

University of Glasgow

universitystory.gla.ac.uk

Browse records of 19,050 graduates of the university, from its foundation in 1451 until 1914.

University of Nottingham Archives

nottingham.ac.uk/manuscriptsandspecialcollections/collectionsindepth/university/introduction.aspx

Oxford University Archives

www.oua.ox.ac.uk

Cambridge University Archives

www.lib.cam.ac.uk/deptserv/manuscripts/

Maybole Ragged School, Ayrshire, Scotland

maybole.org/history/articles/mayboleraggedschool.htm

Berwick County Primary's Log Book

communities.northumberland.gov.uk/Berwick_C13.htm#007829

Online School Registers for County Donegal

freepages.genealogy.rootsweb.ancestry.com/~donegal/school.htm

City of Norwich School Archives

cnsobg.org.uk/archives/

History of Education Society
historyofeducation.org.uk

University of Huddersfield Heritage Quay
heritagequay.org

Childrenshomes
childrenshomes.org.uk

See also: 4.8 Teachers

2.10 Directories

Directories can be very useful for tracing ancestors' whereabouts between census years. They can also be the only source of information for records of small businesses, shops and many other cottage industries that had no centralized administrative body or modern repository.

Historical Directories
specialcollections.le.ac.uk/cdm/landingpage/collection/p16445coll4

Although no longer housed in its original dedicated website, all the digitized trade/street directories (covering areas of England and Wales from the 1760s to the 1910s) are still available via the University of Leicester's Special Collections Online. The directories can be browsed by location and viewed online, or downloaded as a PDF. At the time of writing, the data was due to join the federated search engine ConnectedHistories (connectedhistories.org).

Scottish Post Office Directories, National Library of Scotland
digital.nls.uk/directories/

Free searchable hub to more than 700 digitized directories from the National Library of Scotland, covering most of the country between the years 1773 and 1911. There's also an NLS guide (nls.uk/family-history/directories), which describes the various directories held here – from street directories to military directories.

Directories Index, Sheffield Indexers
sheffieldindexers.com/DirectoriesIndex.html

Launched in 2001, the Sheffield Indexers' mission is to provide accurate indexed transcriptions of genealogical records free of charge. There's all kinds of material here, and this page lists the local directories added to date.

Street Directories, Public Record Office of Northern Ireland
streetdirectories.proni.gov.uk

This is PRONI's dedicated sub-site, where it reproduces a large number of directories from Belfast and environs, dating from 1819 to 1900.

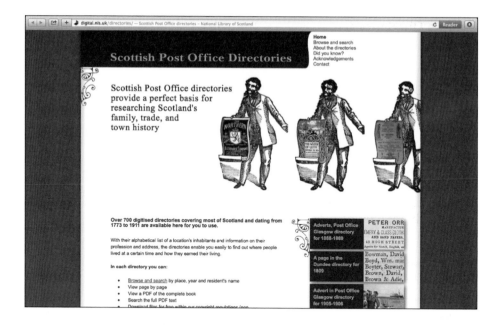

Directories, FamilyRelatives

familyrelatives.com/post_search.php

This site has a large number of directories and periodicals, including a range of 1835 Pigot's directories from across England and Wales.

Addressing History

addressinghistory.edina.ac.uk

Combines data from post office directories from Edinburgh, Glasgow and Aberdeen with historical maps.

Your Old Books and Maps

youroldbooksandmaps.co.uk

Republishes rare books and maps on disc and/or PDF download, including many county directories.

Belfast Directories

www.lennonwylie.co.uk

Transcribed Belfast directories from between 1805 and 1913.

Library Ireland

libraryireland.com

Digitized copies of all kinds of historic volumes, including some directories.

Midlands Historical Data

www.midlandshistoricaldata.org

Offers pay-per-view access to Midlands directories.

Guide to Directories and Periodicals, BBC History

bbc.co.uk/history/familyhistory/next_steps/adv_05_directories_periodicals_01.
shtml

See also: 1.3 The Census, 2.3 Taxation, 2.4 Election Records, 4.19 Other Occupations and Apprentices

2.11 Newspapers

The British Newspaper Archive is the leading commercial website in its field, and offers access to the British Library's newspaper collections. Many current newspapers run their own pay-per-view or subscription archives, plus there are several websites offering at least partial access to national, regional and specialist titles.

British Newspaper Archives

britishnewspaperarchive.co.uk

The British Newspaper Archive is built on collections preserved by the British Library. It tends to expand in fits and starts, hitting milestones such as 7 million pages in 2013, and 9 million in 2014. Additional local newspapers from England, Scotland and Wales were launched during 2015, alongside many more Irish titles. Searching is free, but it costs to view the resulting images, although free access is available in many archives and libraries. You can try to influence which newspapers are digitized next by voting through: help-and-advice.britishnewspaperarchive. co.uk.

Welsh Newspapers Online

papuraunewyddcymru.llgc.org.uk

At the time of writing, this expanding free resource boasted 7.6 million articles on 725,000 pages that are preserved at the National Library of Wales – with 100,000 pages added in a single month. You can search by categories such as family notices and advertisements, and browse by exact date, date range, or by region/title.

Researching Newspapers, British Library guide

bl.uk/help/researching-newspapers

BL guide to researching its holdings produced by the Newspaper Reference Service. Various online collections are at bl.uk/subjects/news-media, where you can also find out more about the Newsroom – the BL's new dedicated newspaper research space in the St Pancras building.

The Gazette

www.thegazette.co.uk

Offers access to the official public record for the London, Edinburgh and Belfast editions. The site has been given a makeover in recent years which enables you to search for specific content such as wills and probate, insolvency and military/ civilian awards – although exploring individual editions is not as simple as it was.

Gale Digital Collections

gdc.gale.com

Home to a huge number of newspaper archives, including the *Daily Mail* and *The Times*; the former BL website, 19th Century British Library Newspapers; and the Burney Collection of seventeenth- and eighteenth-century English newspapers. However these resources are only available for institutions – not for individual subscriptions.

Trove, Australia

trove.nla.gov.au

A fabulous resource for those with Australian interests, Trove offers access to books, images, historic newspapers, maps, music and archives. You can search newspapers by title, date or choose a region.

UK Press Online

ukpressonline.co.uk/ukpressonline/

Gateway to 2 million pages of newspapers including the *Daily Mirror* (from 1903 onwards) and the *Daily Express* (from 1900 onwards). Anyone can search, but will require a subscription to view, download and print.

Scotsman Digital Archive

archive.scotsman.com

Explore issues of the liberal weekly back to its launch in 1817. Two-day unlimited access costs £7.95, a year costs £99.99.

Nineteenth-Century Serials Edition

www.ncse.ac.uk/index.html

Online edition of six titles including Chartist newspaper the *Northern Star* (1838–52), *The Leader* (1950–60) and the *English Woman's Journal* (1858–64).

ConnectedHistories

connectedhistories.org

Federated search hub where you can search British Newspapers 1800–1900 and the seventeenth/eighteenth-century Burney Collection of printed papers.

Word on the Street

digital.nls.uk/broadsides/

National Library of Scotland's online collection of nearly 1,800 broadsides.

Archive

archive.org

Hosts all kinds of digitized periodicals, newspapers and journals, including *The Strand*.

Teesdale Mercury Archive
teesdalemercuryarchive.org.uk
Explore the archives of County Durham's *Teesdale Mercury* 1854–1954.

Guardian and Observer Archive
theguardian.com/gnm-archive
Archive section which also includes brief histories of both titles.

Newspaper Indexes, Highland History and Culture
www.ambaile.org.uk
Indexes to six Scottish newspapers.

The Spectator Archive 1828–2008
archive.spectator.co.uk

The Times Archive
thetimes.co.uk/tto/archive/

Last Chance To Read
lastchancetoread.com

Internet Library of Early Journals
www.bodley.ox.ac.uk/ilej/

Isle of Wight County Press Archive
archive.iwcp.co.uk

Manx National Heritage (1792–1960)
www.imuseum.im

Google News Archive Search
news.google.com/archivesearch

2.12 Migration

Online you can track ocean voyages and cross-border movements, and find social histories of mass migrations, from the Highland clearances to the influx of Huguenot refugees. You'll also find useful research groups and forums dedicated to oversees communities in Britain.

The National Archives, A–Z research guides
nationalarchives.gov.uk/records/atoz/
There are so many TNA guides that touch on the subject of migration it seemed more logical to direct you to the A–Z list, from where you can find Certificates of British Citizenship, Emigrants, Evacuees, Immigrants, Internees, Naturalised Britons, Passengers, Passports and Refugees. Each of these categories will link to

allied guides and show what material is held where, on- and offline – although they're not always bang up to date. You can also search the likes of Naturalisation Case Papers (1789–1934), for example, via TNA catalogue Discovery.

Documenting Ireland: Parliament, People and Migration
www.dippam.ac.uk

A family of sites that together document Irish migration since the eighteenth century. Voices of Migration and Return, and the Irish Emigration Database are based on roughly 33,000 documents – including letters, diaries and journals written by migrants, and newspaper material such as advertisements and overseas BMD notices.

Travel and Migration, Findmypast
search.findmypast.co.uk/search-united-kingdom-records-in-travel-and-migration

From the migration search page you can narrow searches by departure port, destination country/port, or collection. The links sidebar will take you to individual pages such as Passenger Lists Leaving the UK (1890–1960) and Index to Register of Passport Applications (1851–1903) collections.

BMD Registers
bmdregisters.co.uk

Search for official BMD records that might be useful for migrating ancestors such as births, marriages and deaths on British registered ships (1854–91), or foreign registers and returns (1627–1960). It also has non-parochial registers from French, Dutch, German and Swiss churches in London and elsewhere.

Immigration and Travel, Ancestry
search.ancestry.co.uk/search/category.aspx?cat=40

This address takes you to the Immigration and Travel search page, from where you can find key TNA sources that include Alien Arrivals (1810–11, 1826–69); Incoming Passenger Lists (1878–1960); Outgoing Passenger Lists (1890–1960); and Aliens Entry Books (1794–1921).

Immigrant Ships Transcribers Guild
immigrantships.net

The rather confusing layout means it's easiest if you choose one of the volumes near the top of the homepage, then scroll down and pick a departure/arrival point. There's also advice via the Compass section (immigrantships.net/newcompass/pcindex.html).

British Home Children in Canada
canadianbritishhomechildren.weebly.com

History and data relating to approximately 118,000 children sent to Canada from the United Kingdom under the child migration scheme (1863–1939).

Jewish Genealogical Society of Great Britain
jgsgb.org.uk/immigration-and-emigration

Explores Jewish migration to and from the United Kingdom through the ages, plus lots of advice about researching Jewish communities and individuals overseas.

Port Cities Southampton
www.plimsoll.org

The Port Cities family of maritime websites are no longer updated, but you can still find some interesting material about trade, travel by sea and migration.

Highlands and Islands Emigration Society
scan.org.uk/researchrtools/emigration.htm

SCAN page detailing the society that between 1852 and 1857 assisted almost 5,000 individuals to leave western Scotland for Australia.

Scottish Emigration Database
abdn.ac.uk/emigration/

Contains records of 21,000 passengers who embarked from various Scottish ports between 1890 and 1960.

Ellis Island
libertyellisfoundation.org

This completely free database of migrants entering the United States is drawn from passenger lists and ships' manifests.

Castle Garden
castlegarden.org

Before Ellis Island there was Castle Garden, and this site provides a database of 11 million immigrants from 1820 through to 1892.

The Highland Clearances
highlandclearances.co.uk

Explores the causes, story and long-term impact of forced the mass displacement known as the Highland clearances.

Highland Clearances, Electric Scotland
electricscotland.com/history/hclearances.htm

Ads strangle the life out of this website, which has interesting content if you have the patience to find it.

Wall of Honor, The Statue of Liberty and Ellis Island
libertyellisfoundation.org/about-the-wall-of-honor

The American Immigrant Wall of Honor is a permanent exhibit of individual and family names.

The Ships List
theshipslist.com
Wonderful maritime miscellany, including passenger lists from across the globe.

Emigrants From England 1773–76
rootsweb.ancestry.com/~ote/ships/english1773-76a.htm
One of several free UK emigrant lists available via Rootsweb.

Black Presence
nationalarchives.gov.uk/pathways/blackhistory/index.htm
TNA exhibition exploring Asian and black history in Britain, 1500–1850.

Merseyside Maritime Museum
liverpoolmuseums.org.uk/maritime/archive/sheet/10
Information sheet on child migration.

Anglo-German Family History Society
agfhs.org.uk

Huguenot Society of Great Britain and Ireland
huguenotsociety.org.uk

Huguenot Museum
www.frenchhospital.org.uk/huguenot-museum/

Black Cultural Archives
bcaheritage.org.uk

Immigrants to Canada in the Nineteenth Century
jubilation.uwaterloo.ca/~marj/genealogy/thevoyage.html

Child Migrants Trust
childmigrantstrust.com

Migration Heritage Australia
migrationheritage.nsw.gov.au

The Mayflower Society
themayflowersociety.com

Families in British India Society
fibis.org

India Office Family Search, British Library
indiafamily.bl.uk/UI/

BMDs on Royal Navy and Merchant Ships (1794–1972), Findmypast
search.findmypast.co.uk/search-world-records/births-at-sea-1854-1960

Australian Migration and Citizenship, National Archives of Australia
naa.gov.au/collection/explore/migration/index.aspx

Aliens' Registration Cards 1918–1957, The National Archives
nationalarchives.gov.uk/records/aliens-registration-cards.htm

British Overseas Records, Family Relatives
familyrelatives.com/information/info_detail.php?id=100

British Nationals Born Overseas 1818–2005, Findmypast
search.findmypast.co.uk/search-united-kingdom-records/british-nationals-born-overseas-1818-2005

See also: 2.13 Overseas Research, 4.5 Merchant Navy, 4.16 East India Company

2.13 Overseas Research

If you're researching your family's overseas origins, or perhaps individuals who spent time living and working abroad, you will need to familiarize yourself with local sources and archives. Below are a handful of useful general resource sites to get you started, plus some important overseas collections.

Convicts to Australia
members.iinet.net.au/~perthdps/convicts/

This site offers all kinds of free datasets and primary/secondary sources relating to transportation to Australia, including transcribed lists of the First, Second and Third Fleets; you will also find information about individual ships, such as ports of departure and arrival, and various crew/convict lists. There's an excellent links section with details of key state and national archives.

Jewish Genealogical Society of Great Britain
jgsgb.org.uk

One of the most highly respected genealogical societies in the country. There seem to be occasional caching issues with the homepage, so you could go direct to the Immigration and Emigration section at: jgsgb.org.uk/immigration-and-emigration.

Cyndi's List
cyndislist.com

The links hub really comes into its own if you're researching overseas. Click Categories and you'll find sections on Belgium (187 sites listed); France (590); Italy (492); Baltic States (226); Africa (126); and of course the United States (167,636).

Huguenot Society
huguenotsociety.org.uk

Founded by the directors of the French Hospital in 1885, the bicentenary year of the Revocation of the Edict of Nantes, to promote the publication and interchange of knowledge about the Huguenots in Great Britain and Ireland.

US Immigrant Ancestors Project

immigrants.byu.edu

The Immigrant Ancestors Project is sponsored by the Center for Family History and Genealogy at Brigham Young University. It uses emigration registers to locate information about the birthplaces of immigrants in their native countries.

Overseas Repositories, The National Archives

discover.nationlarchives.gov.uk/find-an-archive

List of overseas repositories noted in the National Register of Archives. There's also the general emigration research guide at: nationalarchives.gov.uk/records/research-guides/emigration.htm.

Families in British India Society

fibis.org

Home to lots of advice for tracing family members overseas, plus a database of nearly 1.5 million names and the expanding Fibiwiki at: wiki.fibis.org/index.php/Main_Page.

British Library India Office Collection

indiafamily.bl.uk/ui/home.aspx

Much of the key material held here is now available through Findmypast (findmypast.co.uk/articles/world-records/search-all-uk-records/special-collections/british-india-office-collection).

Anglo-German Family History Society

agfhs.org.uk

Aimed at researchers tracing individuals from German-speaking parts of Europe who settled in the UK.

Immigrant Ships Transcribers Guild

immigrantships.net

Slowly expanding database of transcribed passenger lists that can be searched by port of arrival or departure.

National Archives, America

archives.gov

The home page of America's National Archives, plus there's a directory of state-level archives at archives.gov/research/alic/reference/state-archives.html.

National Archives of Australia

naa.gov.au

Library and Archives Canada

bac-lac.gc.ca/eng

Archives New Zealand
archives.govt.nz

Ellis Island
libertyellisfoundation.org

The Ships List
theshipslist.com

See also: 2.12 Migration, 5.1 Resources by Region

2.14 Wales

While there are some unique problems facing researchers with Welsh interests, once you've grappled with the patronymic naming system you'll soon discover that there are also a number of very useful and freely available resources aimed at family historians.

The National Library of Wales
llgc.org.uk

The recently tablet-optimized homepage boasts some of the library's vital statistics – 950,000 photographs, 1.5 million maps, 5 million digital images and e-resources and 15km of archives. Start by clicking Collections > Archives to read about major collections such as the Church in Wales Archive, which preserves registers of baptisms, marriages and burials, bishop's transcripts, wills and marriage bonds. The site also has several expanding and completed databases – you can, for example, search and view wills proved in the Welsh ecclesiastical courts before 1858 via cat.llgc.org.uk/probate.

The Wales Collections, Findmypast
findmypast.co.uk/articles/world-records/search-all-uk-records/special-collections/the-wales-collection

The National Library of Wales/Welsh County Archivists Group are collaborating with Findmypast on the Wales Collection, which includes several million parish records covering Anglesey, Breconshire (Brecknockshire), Caernarvonshire, Cardiganshire, Carmarthenshire, Denbighshire, Flintshire, Glamorganshire, Merionethshire, Monmouthshire, Montgomeryshire, Pembrokeshire and Radnorshire.

Welsh Newspapers Online
welshnewspapers.llgc.org.uk

It is hoped that the National Library of Wales' fantastic free newspaper resource will soon hit 1 million pages. It already boasts a huge range of Welsh and English-language titles published between 1804 and 1919, and search tools include the ability to narrow results to family notices and announcements.

Archives Wales

archiveswales.org.uk

Federated catalogue that holds information from more than 7,000 collections across twenty-one archives in Wales. There are advice pages aimed at beginners, a handy Find Your Archive drop-down menu, plus lots of news on digitization projects.

CYMRU 1914

cymru1914.org

Centenary project that is seeing the mass digitization of sources relating to the First World War – from libraries, special collections and archives across Wales. Material includes newspapers, archives and manuscripts, photographs, journals and sound recordings.

Welsh Coal Mines

welshcoalmines.co.uk

This site catalogues mines situated within Welsh coalfields, with histories, photographs, poems and stories from the once-dominant industry. There's also a List of Disasters, which documents more than 6,000 mining accidents where there were 5 or more fatalities.

Cynefin: A Sense of Place

cynefin.archiveswales.org.uk

Recently launched website which hosts all 1,200 sheets of the Welsh tithe maps, and covers about 95 per cent of the country. The accompanying apportionment documents are being transcribed by volunteers.

Wales, Genuki

genuki.org.uk/big/wal/

A good place to familiarize yourself with Welsh genealogy, with county-by-county guides to resources, societies, archives and possible pitfalls caused by shifting boundaries and the Welsh naming system.

North Wales BMD

northwalesbmd.org.uk

Collaboration between three genealogical groups and local registration services to provide free BMD indexes (1837–1950) for the area. Last updated in 2012, it contains 1,347,130 births; 435,103 marriages; and 794,517 deaths.

Welsh Naming, BBC Family History

bbc.co.uk/wales/history/sites/themes/society/family_03_welshnaming.shtml

Archived section of BBC Cymru's History section, which introduces the ancient Welsh patronymic naming system, and the problems it can cause genealogists.

Welsh Mariners

welshmariners.org.uk

An online index of around 23,500 Welsh merchant mariners active between 1800 and 1945.

People's Collection Wales

peoplescollectionwales.co.uk

Photographs, sound recordings, documents, videos and stories from museums and archives.

Quick Research Links, FamilySearch

familysearch.org/learn/wiki/en/Quick_Research_Links_-_Wales

Lists parish and other Welsh collections that are available by county.

Cymru'n Cofio/Wales Remembers 1914–1918

walesremembers.org

Official First World War centenary hub.

Digging up the Past

diggingupthepast.org.uk

Photographs documenting mining in south Wales.

Pembrokeshire Archives

www.pembrokeshire.gov.uk/content.asp?nav=107,1447

Recently opened in its new home in Haverfordwest.

Gwent Archives

gwentarchives.gov.uk

Opened its new site in Ebbw Vale in 2011.

Gwynedd Archives Service
gwynedd.gov.uk/archives
Runs the Caernarvon and Meirionnydd Record Offices.

UK Genealogy Online, Wales
uk-genealogy-online.com/wales.html

Welsh Family History Archive
jlb2011.co.uk/wales/

Wales Gen Web Project
www.walesgenweb.com

Association of Family History Societies of Wales
fhswales.org.uk

Powys County Archives
powys.gov.uk/en/archives/find-archives-local-records/

Glamorgan Archives
glamarchives.gov.uk

West Glamorgan Archive Service
swansea.gov.uk/westglamorganarchives

Anglesey Records and Archives
www.anglesey.gov.uk/leisure/records-and-archives/

Ceredigion Archives
archifdy-ceredigion.org.uk

Carmarthenshire Archives Service
www.carmarthenshire.gov.uk/english/leisure/archives/pages/archivesrecords.aspx

Denbighshire Archives
www.denbighshire.gov.uk/en/resident/libraries-and-archives/denbighshire-archives/denbighshire-archives.aspx

Flintshire Record Office
www.flintshire.gov.uk/en/LeisureAndTourism/Records-and-Archives/Home.aspx

Cardiganshire FHS
cgnfhs.org.uk

Clwyd FHS
clwydfhs.org.uk

Dyfed FHS
dyfedfhs.org.uk

Glamorgan FHS
glamfhs.org.uk

Gwent FHS
gwentfhs.info

Gwynedd FHS
gwyneddfhs.org

Montgomeryshire Genealogical Society
montgomeryshiregs.org.uk

Powys FHS
powysfhs.org.uk

See also: 4.1 Miners, 5.1 Resources by Region

2.15 Ireland

While you can't escape the catastrophic loss of census material in the Four Courts fire of June 1922, the practical upshot is that a huge quantity of very useful census substitute sources have been indexed, transcribed, digitized and placed online.

National Archive of Ireland

nationalarchives.ie

Follow the family history signpost to view collection highlights, or go direct to the specialist genealogy site (genealogy.nationalarchives.ie) where you can access all kinds of digital resources such as the Soldiers' Wills database (Irish soldiers who died while serving in the British army during the First World War); Tithe Applotment Books; census search forms (1841–51) and the censuses of Ireland (see below); and the Calendars of Wills and Administrations (1858–1922). Digitized Irish Catholic parish registers were to be launched mid-2015.

Public Record Office of Northern Ireland

www.proni.gov.uk

The PRONI site is dated, but it provides plenty of important finding aids and free material. There are also advice pages, guides, and an increasing number of images and other collections' highlights, which are available through third-party sites such as Flickr. Online records include the Ulster Covenant (containing the signatures of 237,368 men and 234,046 women, from September 1912) and records of freeholders (lists of people eligible to vote). There's also an index to will calendar entries from the District Probate Registries of Armagh, Belfast and Londonderry.

Derry Genealogy Centre

derrycity.gov.uk/Genealogy/Derry-Genealogy

Details of a mass index to pre-1922 civil birth and marriage registers; early BMD registers of eighty-five churches (twenty-six Roman Catholic Church, twenty-four Church of Ireland and thirty-five Presbyterian); and gravestone inscriptions from 117 graveyards. Searches are free via derry.rootsireland.ie; viewing records is on a pay-per-view basis.

Griffith's Valuation

askaboutireland.ie/griffith-valuation

Provides free online access to various sources including Griffith's Valuation, the full-scale valuation of property in Ireland, which was overseen by Richard Griffith and published county by county between 1847 and 1864. 'The only comprehensive … account of where people lived in mid-nineteenth century Ireland. It covers over a million dwellings, and nearly 20 million acres, recording around 80 per cent of the population.'

Ireland, Civil Registration Indexes, 1845–1958, FamilySearch

familysearch.org/search/collection/1408347

This FamilySearch page details Irish civil registrations indexes. You can also scroll down to explore other Irish collections available, or there's the Ireland Wiki page at familysearch.org/learn/wiki/en/Ireland, which leads to major parish collections, prison registers, tithe applotments and more.

Belfast City Council Burial Records

belfastcity.gov.uk/community/burialrecords/burialrecords.aspx

Search through 360,000 records from Belfast City Cemetery, Roselawn Cemetery and Dundonald Cemetery. The database gives name, age, last place of residence, sex, date of birth, date of burial, cemetery, grave section and number. You can buy images of burial records that are over 75 years old for £1.50 each.

1901/1911 Census, National Archive of Ireland

census.nationalarchives.ie

Home to the aforementioned 1901 and 1911 census material for all thirty-two counties, and searchable by all the information categories. You can also read more about the surviving census fragments and census substitutes for 1821 and 1851.

National Museums Northern Ireland

nmni.com/home.aspx

Home of the Ulster Museum, the Ulster Folk and Transport Museum, the Ulster American Folk Park and the Armagh County Museum. The Collections Search currently allows you to explore artefacts, photographs and various documents online.

Centre for Migration Studies

qub.ac.uk/cms/

The Centre for Migration Studies in Omagh has created an Irish Emigration Database containing 33,000 primary source documents on all aspects of Irish emigration to North America, going back to the early 1700s.

Documenting Ireland

www.dippam.ac.uk

A family of heritage websites that include Enhanced British Parliamentary Papers on Ireland – a collection of 15,000 official publications from the period of the Union – and the Voices of Migration and Return, based around interviews with Ulster migrants.

Military Archives

www.militaryarchives.ie

Official home of the records of the Department of Defence, the Defence Forces and the Army Pensions Board. Has lots of online collections including the Military Service Pension Collection 1916–23.

Irish Genealogy

irishgenealogy.ie

Home to online indexes of the civil registers (GRO) of births, marriages, civil partnerships and deaths and to church records of baptism, marriage and burial from a number of counties.

Treaty Exhibition

treaty.nationalarchives.ie

Site created to focus on the ninetieth anniversary of the signing of the Anglo-Irish Treaty of 1921. The core is the original document itself released online in its entirety in December 2011.

National Library of Ireland

www.nli.ie

You can explore various family history sources via the online catalogue, plus there's a newspaper database, a sources database, manuscript collection lists and digital photographs.

Townlands Index, Irish Ancestors

irishancestors.ie/?page_id=5392

Ireland has more than 64,000 townlands, the most basic unit of land division in the country. This index shows which civil parish each townland would have belonged to.

The Linen Hall Library, Belfast

linenhall.com

Houses genealogical material, including the Blackwood Pedigrees (a collection of over 1,000 manuscript family trees) plus parish registers.

Diamond War Memorial, Derry

diamondwarmemorial.com

Project in which a local historian has uncovered around 400 names that had been overlooked from the Diamond War Memorial in Derry.

Irish Ancestors

irishancestors.ie/?page_id=1514

This is the Irish Ancestors census advice page, an example of some of the beginners' guidance available here.

RootsIreland

rootsireland.ie

This site also contains birth, marriage, death and gravestone records, the majority of which are only available via this website.

Jewish Communities and Records (JCR-UK)

jewishgen.org/jcr-uk

JewishGen/JGSGB is a project that records communities/congregations in the UK and the Republic of Ireland.

Property Registration Authority

www.prai.ie

The Registry of Deeds holds more than 5 million memorials (summaries of deeds) from 1708 to the present day.

Street Directories, Public Record Office of Northern Ireland

streetdirectories.proni.gov.uk

Freely accessible digitized street directories covering Belfast and the surrounding area (1819–1900).

Eddies Extracts

freepages.genealogy.rootsweb.ancestry.com/~econnolly/

Names of over 25,000 Presbyterians who served during the First World War.

Placenamesni.org

www.placenamesni.org

The origins and meanings of more than 30,000 place names in Northern Ireland.

GRONI, General Register Office Northern Ireland

nidirect.gov.uk/family-history

Access to Northern Irish birth, marriage and death records online.

1901 census for Leitrim and Roscommon

leitrim-roscommon.com/1901census/

Also covers parts of Mayo, Sligo, Wexford, Westmeath and Galway.

Irelands, Ancestry

ancestry.co.uk/cs/uk/ireland

Includes Irish Roman Catholic registers 1763–1912.

Discovereverafter

discovereverafter.com

Irish burial/MI data for genealogists.

Irish Ancestors, Irish Times

irishtimes.com/ancestor

Emerald Ancestors

emeraldancestors.com

Ulster Historical Foundation

ancestryireland.com

Library Ireland

libraryireland.com

Irish Genealogical Research Society

igrsoc.org

Irish Ancestral Research Association

tiara.ie

Irish Family History Society
ifhs.ie

Association of Professional Genealogists in Ireland
apgi.ie

Presbyterian Historical Society of Ireland
presbyterianhistoryireland.com

Irish Railway Record Society
www.irrs.ie

Genealogical Society of Ireland
familyhistory.ie

Belfast Street Directories
lennonwylie.co.uk

Irish Family History Foundation
irish-roots.ie

Corpus of Electronic Texts
www.ucc.ie/celt/

Belfast Central Library
www.librariesni.org.uk

North of Ireland Family History Society
nifhs.org

Trinity College, Dublin
tcd.ie

Eneclann
eneclann.ie

Findmypast
findmypast.ie

See also: 2.12 Migration, 4.3 Railways, 5.1 Resources by Region

2.16 Scotland

Scotland has spent much of the last two decades leading the way in terms of online genealogy. While some key resources are beginning to look a little old-fashioned, there's a huge amount you can achieve online, plus many websites where you can familiarize yourself with some of the subtleties (and advantages) of Scottish genealogical records.

National Records of Scotland

nrscotland.gov.uk

In 2011 the General Register Office for Scotland (gro-scotland.gov.uk) merged with the National Archives of Scotland (nas.gov.uk) to become the National Records of Scotland (NRS). Both old websites remain online, but were slowly being mothballed at the time of writing. As the umbrella organization, NRS is responsible for Scottish government records back to the twelfth century; law, church, business and estate records; statutory registers; and the census.

ScotlandsPeople

scotlandspeople.gov.uk

The single most important web resource for Scottish research, boasting more than 90 million records. There's a credits system for accessing the material, which includes statutory BMD registers, OPRs (old parish registers), Catholic registers, census records, valuation rolls, plus soldiers' wills, wills and testaments, and coats of arms. A good jumping-off point for beginners is About our records > Record examples.

National Library of Scotland

www.nls.uk

Preserves enormous amounts of genealogically useful material, from newspapers, electoral registers, maps and military listings to emigration passenger lists dating from the mid-sixteenth century. Of the many highlights, try nls.uk/maps, where you can zoom in, pan out and print historic maps from all over Scotland.

Scottish Mining

scottishmining.co.uk

Explores the history of Scottish mining through old reports, gazetteers and newspaper articles. It's both a social history of the subject and a useful work of reference, with histories of individual mining parishes; more than 22,000 names of those involved in the coal, iron and shale mining industries; plus an accident database.

Glasgow Family History, Mitchell Library

glasgowfamilyhistory.org.uk

Wonderful website for the Mitchell Library in Glasgow, which features burial records, BMD data, census material and details of the First World War *Evening Times* roll of honour. Plus there's a complete A–Z of research guides. You can also explore some image collections via the old mitchelllibrary.org/virtualmitchell/.

British Newspaper Archive

britishnewspaperarchive.co.uk

Has lots of national and regional newspapers for Scotland. For example, new titles added towards the end of 2014 included the *Aberdeen Journal* and the *Arbroath Herald and Advertiser*. From the home page you can browse by place of publication: choose a county from the drop-down menu or click on the map.

National Archives of Scotland
nas.gov.uk

As mentioned above, this site is at an in-between stage as content migrates to the NRS website, but in the meantime there's still lots of useful material here – not least the record guides at nas.gov.uk/guides/default.asp.

FamilySearch
familysearch.org

The free searchable database includes the International Genealogical Index, which has lots of information drawn from OPRs. To see the full range of Scottish resources go to: familysearch.org/learn/wiki/en/Scotland.

ScotlandsPlaces
scotlandsplaces.gov.uk

Digitized historical resources relating to places throughout Scotland. These include all kinds of historical tax rolls and Ordnance Survey books, which are accessible with a subscription.

ScotlandsPeople Centre
scotlandspeoplehub.gov.uk

Find out more about using the ScotlandsPeople research centre in Edinburgh. This site is also moving to the National Records of Scotland website (nrscotland.gov.uk).

The Scotsman Archive
archive.scotsman.com

The Scotsman was founded in 1817 and here you can search a complete digital archive of the newspaper up to 1950. You can pay for one day's access or an annual subscription.

National Register of Archives for Scotland
nas.gov.uk/nras/

Searchable register of collections held by private individuals and families, landed estates, clubs and societies, businesses and law firms.

Addressing History
addressinghistory.edina.ac.uk

Explore data drawn from post office directories from Edinburgh (1784–5, 1865, 1881, 1891, 1905–6), Glasgow (1881, 1891) and Aberdeen (1881, 1891).

Historic Hospital Admission Records Project
hharp.org

Database of patients' names in 120,000 admission records from hospitals in London and Glasgow, including the Royal Hospital for Sick Children in Glasgow (1883–1903).

Statistical Accounts of Scotland 1791–1845
stat-acc-scot.edina.ac.uk/sas/sas.asp?action=public

Explore the 'Old' (1791–99) and 'New' (1834–45) statistical accounts of Scotland. The site offers parish-by-parish reports for the whole of Scotland.

Scottish Catholic Archives
scottishcatholicarchives.org.uk

Information about the holdings of the Scottish Catholic Archives, including a list of parish registers held here.

British GENES blog
britishgenes.blogspot.com

Chris Paton's blog is a bustling one-man newswire service, with lots of attention devoted to Scottish genealogy.

Scottish Handwriting
scottishhandwriting.com

Online tuition to help researchers read and interpret Scottish records back to the sixteenth century.

Lothian Health Services Archives
www.lhsa.lib.ed.ac.uk

Resources include the Leith Roll of Honour, which lists officers and men killed in the First World War.

Glasgow Story

www.theglasgowstory.co.uk

Dated but interesting website, through which you can also search the 1913–14 Valuation Rolls.

Working-Class Marriage in Scotland, 1855–1976

workingclassmarriage.gla.ac.uk

Academic study, with a gallery of wedding photographs from the mid-nineteenth century through to the 1970s.

University of Glasgow

universitystory.gla.ac.uk

Browse records of 19,050 graduates of the university from its foundation in 1451.

Scottish Emigration Database

www.abdn.ac.uk/emigration/

University of Aberdeen's Scottish Emigration Database.

Scottish Register of Tartans

tartanregister.gov.uk

Explore the database of tartan designs, maintained by the National Records of Scotland.

Scottish Indexes

scottishindexes.com

Has indexes to various record sets at the National Records of Scotland.

Scottish Archive Network

scan.org.uk

A single catalogue to records from fifty-two Scottish archives.

Scottish Screen Archive

ssa.nls.uk

Business Archives Council of Scotland

www.gla.ac.uk/services/archives/bacs/

Scottish Jewish Archives Centre

www.sjac.org.uk

Edinburgh City Libraries

www.capitalcollections.org.uk

Glasgow City Archives

glasgowlife.org.uk/libraries/the-mitchell-library/archives/Pages/home.aspx

TNA Guide – Scotland
nationalarchives.gov.uk/records/looking-for-
person/bmdscotlandandireland.htm

Scottish Genealogy Society
scotsgenealogy.com

Scotland BDM Exchange
sctbdm.com

Scottish Association of Family History Societies
safhs.org.uk

Anglo-Scottish FHS
anglo-scots.mlfhs.org.uk

The Highland Clearances
theclearances.org

Jura Oral History
juradevelopment.co.uk/oral-history-project/

Old Occupations in Scotland
scotsfamily.com/occupations.htm

Highland Memorial Inscriptions
sites.google.com/site/highlandmemorialinscriptions/home

RBS Heritage Hub
heritagearchives.rbs.com

2.17 Hospitals and Medicine

In Section 4 (Occupations) there's a chapter dedicated to finding records of practising doctors and nurses. Here the focus is on hospitals and other institutions of care: their patients, and the wider history of medicine – from the licensed apothecary to the practising surgeon, from the almshouse to the specialist ward.

The Wellcome Library
wellcomelibrary.org

The Wellcome Library is a public venue developed by the Wellcome Trust, which looks after more than 750,000 books and journals; plus manuscripts, archives and films; and more than 250,000 paintings, prints and drawings. Collections are broadly divided into Archives and Manuscripts, History of Medicine Collection and the Medical Collection. There's a catalogue and you can visit Digital Collections to explore the likes of London's Pulse: Medical Officer of Health Reports, 1848–1972. For latest news try the library blog at blog.wellcomelibrary.org, which also has archived articles back to 2008.

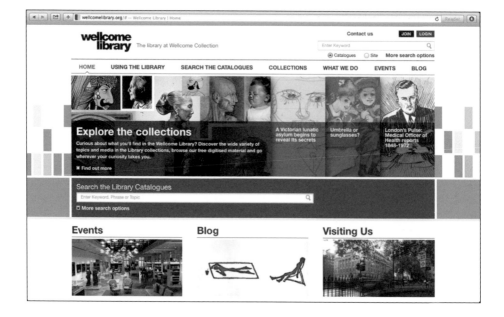

The Wellcome Trust

wellcome.ac.uk

Parent website for the trust, and the body behind many major digitization projects mentioned above. It's currently teaming up with a number of archives across the UK to digitize records of psychiatric hospitals dating back to the eighteenth century. There's also the Wellcome Collection (wellcomecollection.org), home to events, exhibitions and history projects. At the time of writing the lead item was: 'Mindcraft: Explore a century of madness, murder and mental healing.'

Hospital Records Database

nationalarchives.gov.uk/hospitalrecords

Maintained by the Wellcome Library and The National Archives, the Hospital Records Database provides information about the existence and location of the records of UK hospitals. (The majority have been transferred to local record offices or are still administered by health authority archivists.) It also indicates the existence of lists, catalogues or other finding aids.

HHARP

hharp.org

Database of patients in 120,000 admission records of hospitals in London and Glasgow between 1852 and 1914. Included are the Royal Hospital for Sick Children in Glasgow; Great Ormond Street Hospital; the Evelina Hospital; and the Alexandra Hospital for Children with Hip Disease.

Lothian Health Services Archives

lhsa.lib.ed.ac.uk

Alongside records of patients, nurses, doctors and other hospital workers, the archives, which is part-funded by the Wellcome Trust, preserves clinical and non-clinical records dating back to 1770 and 1594 respectively. There is also a 40,000-strong photographic collection.

St Bartholomew's Museum

bartshealth.nhs.uk/bartsmuseum

Set in the historic North Wing of St Bartholomew's Hospital, the museum tells the story of this renowned institution, celebrates its achievements and explains its place in history.

UK Medical Heritage Library

archive.org/details/ukmhl

Expanding collection of freely available digitized books from the Wellcome Library's historical collections, published between 1800 and 1900.

Great Ormond Street Hospital

gosh.nhs.uk/about-us/our-history/archive-service/

Great Ormond Street Hospital's archive contains documents, photographs and artefacts spanning its 160-year history.

Hospitals, Findmypast

findmypast.co.uk/articles/world-records/search-all-uk-records/institution-and-organisation—records/hospitals

Includes Prestwich Asylum Admissions (1851–1901), Salisbury Infirmary Admissions and Discharges (1761–1832) and Bethlem Royal Hospital Admission Records and Casebooks (1728–93).

Royal College of Surgeons, Museum and Archives

rcseng.ac.uk/museums

Includes details of Hunterian Museum collections, which were first brought together by surgeon and anatomist John Hunter (1728–93).

Forces War Records

forces-war-records.co.uk

Recently released a collection of First World War Military Hospitals Admissions and Discharge Registers.

Fair Mile Hospital 1870–2003

berkshirerecordoffice.org.uk/albums/fair-mile-hospital/

Tells the story of the former county lunatic asylum for Berkshire.

St Pancras Almshouses, History
stpancrasalmshouses.org
Has samples that include reports, images and residents recorded in the 1861 census.

Almshouse Project, The Family and Community Historical Research Society
fachrs.com
Society researching almshouse provision from 1500 to 1914.

Buildings History
buildinghistory.org/buildings/charities.shtml
Guide to records of almshouses, workhouses and hospitals.

Wellcome Images
wellcomeimages.org
The Wellcome Trust's online image library.

Worshipful Society of Apothecaries
apothecaries.org
Incorporated as a City Livery Company in 1617.

Old Operating Theatre Museum
thegarret.org.uk

The Foundling Museum
foundlingmuseum.org.uk

Anaesthesia Heritage Centre
aagbi.org

Museum of the Order of St John
museumstjohn.org.uk

St John's Hospital, Bath
stjohnsbath.org.uk/about-st-johns/our-history/

Science Museum, Hospitals Gallery
sciencemuseum.org.uk/broughttolife/themes/hospitals.aspx

Oxfordshire Health Archives
oxfordshirehealtharchives.nhs.uk

Voluntary Hospitals Database
hospitalsdatabase.lshtm.ac.uk

Royal College of Nursing Archives
archives.rcn.org.uk

Royal Albert Hospital Archive
unlockingthepast.org.uk

Huguenot Museum
frenchhospital.org.uk

Medical Museums
medicalmuseums.org

See also: 4.10 Doctors and Nurses

2.18 Catholic Records

Thanks to widespread persecution, it only became commonplace for Catholic records to be maintained from the mid-nineteenth century. However, lots of early material still survives, and registers often give more detail than their Anglican counterparts. It's also important to keep in mind that Catholics frequently appear in Anglican sources.

Catholic National Library
catholic-library.org.uk

Most mission registers (listing baptisms, confirmations, marriages, deaths) remain in the custody of parish priests, but many have been transcribed and indexed by the Catholic FHS and deposited here. The website has a page listing county-by-county coverage of all the registers, plus there's an online catalogue.

Roman Catholic Records, BMD Registers
bmdregisters.co.uk

The official home to TNA's nonconformist holdings, brought to you by TheGenealogist team. It includes Roman Catholic BMD Records from RG4: registers from some Catholic communities in Dorset, Hampshire, Lancashire, Lincolnshire, Northumberland, Nottinghamshire, Oxfordshire and Yorkshire.

Catholic Registers, ScotlandsPeople
scotlandspeople.gov.uk

Click the relevant title on the left-hand menu to explore the Catholic registers available here – which cover all Scottish parishes in existence by 1855. While you will have to register and pay, there's background information and interesting sample documents while you think about taking the plunge.

Birmingham Archdiocesan Archives
birminghamarchdiocesanarchives.org.uk

An example of a Roman Catholic archdiocesan archive. It is the repository for all parishes in the Archdiocese – comprising Staffordshire, Warwickshire, Worcestershire and Oxfordshire. There are currently 55,628 records in the searchable online index.

Catholic Registers, Society of Genealogists

sog.org.uk/search-records/search-sog-data-online/

Looks after some transcribed/indexed Catholic registers. Plus the Data Online section includes an Index of Catholic Nuns 1598–1914. You can search for free, but you will need to be a member to see the results.

Roman Catholic Records, GenGuide

genguide.co.uk/source/roman-catholic-registers-and-records/30/

Useful summary of some of the most important sources available. It gives background to the likes of recusant rolls and returns of papists, before listing websites, CDs, books and online databases (free and pay-to-view).

FamilySearch

familysearch.org

All marriages between 1754 and 1837 had to be Church of England to be legally valid, so you may be able to find records via FamilySearch. (For more sources see chapter 1.4 Parish Registers.)

National Library of Ireland

www.nli.ie/en/parish-register.aspx

This page details the library's Catholic parish register collections, with PDF guides to parishes covered. At the time of writing, this was due to be digitized and launched online in mid-2015.

Liverpool Collection, Ancestry

ancestry.co.uk/dynamic/liverpool

This site has various UK Catholic collections, including this example relating to Liverpool. The site also has several Irish Roman Catholic record sets spanning 1763 to 1912.

Catholic FHS

www.catholic-history.org.uk/cfhs/

Details of society projects and publications; lists of the transcriptions and indexes; plus there's a blog at: catholicfhs.wordpress.com.

Catholic Research Guide, The National Archives

nationalarchives.gov.uk/records/research-guides/catholics.htm

Concise introduction which gives context to the various records, explains the material preserved here (RG4), and details other places to look.

Scottish Catholic Archives

scottishcatholicarchives.org.uk

Official home of the Scottish Catholic Archives in Edinburgh. In the Family History drop-down menu you'll find a list of parish registers.

Durham Records Online

durhamrecordsonline.com

Includes transcripts from Roman Catholic registers covering County Durham and Northumberland. Uses a credits system to charge for the material.

Irish Ancestors

irishtimes.com/ancestor/browse/records/church/catholic/

Commercial site with a large database of material and a useful parish map of Roman Catholic records.

Manchester and Lancashire FHS

mlfhs.org.uk/data/catholic_search.php

Search the society's index to Catholic parish registers for Manchester.

Free Welsh Genealogy

sites.google.com/site/rhopk24324/home

Access to digital copies of Catholic Record Society publications covering Wales.

Catholic Encyclopaedia

newadvent.org/cathen/

American site holding transcribed information from the *Catholic Encyclopaedia*.

Durham County Record Office

www.durhamrecordoffice.org.uk/Pages/RomanCatholicChurches.aspx

Information about Roman Catholic churches and Catholic records in Durham County Record Office.

Catholic Church for England and Wales

catholic-ew.org.uk

Useful for tracking down details of diocesan archives.

Cheshire Nonconformist and Roman Catholic Registers, Findmypast

search.findmypast.co.uk/search-world-records/cheshire-non-conformist-and-roman-catholic-registers-marriages-17th-century-1910

Local Catholic Church Research Guide

localcatholic.webs.com

Leeds Diocesan Archives

dioceseofleeds.org.uk/archives/

See also: 1.4 Parish Registers, 2.20 Nonconformist

2.19 Jewish Records

There's a whole family of Jewish websites that are particularly valuable for researching Jewish ancestry in Britain, plus global bodies whose online presence is dedicated to recording and honouring the victims of the Holocaust.

Jewish Communities and Records (JCR-UK)
jewishgen.org/jcr-uk

Joint JewishGen and JGSGB project that records Jewish communities/congregations in the UK, Republic of Ireland and Gibraltar. The All-UK Database search page holds more than 300,000 records, including the updated 1851 Anglo-Jewry Database, which covers about 90 per cent of Jews living in the British Isles in 1851 (29,000 entries).

Jewish Genealogical Society of Great Britain
jgsgb.org.uk

Contains databases, research tips, FAQs, news and publications. Lots of the material is only available to members (£35 at time of writing), but the Resources drop-down menu takes you to all kinds of useful material. Plus the Latest News sidebar often details new digitizations available through the society's JCR-UK collaboration with JewishGen.

The Knowles Collection, FamilySearch
familysearch.org/learn/wiki/en/The_Knowles_collection:_the_Jews_of_the_British_Isles

Free database of Jewish records from the British Isles. The collection links together into family groups thousands of individual Jews (over 191,000 as of April 2014). Includes BMD material from the Bevis Marks Synagogue and the Great Synagogue of London, plus cemetery records from London and Manchester.

Jews and Jewish Communities Guide, The National Archives
nationalarchives.gov.uk/records/research-guides/anglo-jewish-history-18th-20th.htm

A good thumbnail introduction to the subject, linking to some of the most important online sources. Via Discovery you can download the likes of surviving aliens' registration cards for the London area (1918–57), and denization and naturalization case papers (HO 1) for 1801 to 1871, plus you can use Discovery to trawl material held elsewhere.

Jewish Collections, Ancestry
ancestry.com/jewishgen-all

Ancestry's American Jewish research landing page. This is a collaboration between JewishGen, the American Jewish Joint Distribution Committee, the American Jewish Historical Society and The Miriam Weiner Routes to Roots Foundation 'to create the world's largest online collection of Jewish historical records'.

British-Jewry
british-jewry.org.uk

Home of the British-Jewry mailing list, with advice, tools, finding aids and databases. For example, the Leeds Database section (british-jewry.org.uk/leedsjewry/) draws on the census, absent voter's lists, burial/marriage collections, *Jewish Chronicle* notices, items from the *London Gazette* and naturalizations.

JewishGen
jewishgen.org

Free registration allows access to many valuable resources. There's the Family-Finder which gives surnames and ancestral towns of more than 500,000 entries, while the Burial Registry has more than 2 million entries from 4,200 cemeteries in 83 countries.

Yad Vashem
yadvashem.org/yv/en/remembrance/names/index.asp

Working to recover the names of the 6 million Jews who perished in the Holocaust. To date, around 4 million are memorialized in Yad Vashem's central database of Holocaust victims.

Judaica Europeana
judaica-europeana.eu

Part of the Europeana project, providing digital access to treasures from libraries, archives and museums across Europe. Led by the European Association for Jewish Culture (jewishcultureineurope.org).

Jewish holdings guide, London Metropolitan Archives
www.cityoflondon.gov.uk/things-to-do/visiting-the-city/archives-and-city-history/london-metropolitan-archives/the-collections/Pages/jewish-life.aspx

The downloadable leaflet on this page is the easiest way to explore the important Jewish collections held at the London Metropolitan Archives.

Jewish Heritage UK
jewish-heritage-uk.org

Dedicated to the architecture of the Jewish Community – includes a directory of listed synagogues across the UK.

Anglo-Jewish Miscellanies
jeffreymaynard.com

A collection of historical and genealogical information about the Jewish community in England.

Jewish East End
jewisheastend.com/london.html

This site has historic and contemporary photos of Jewish synagogues and cemeteries in East End London.

Jewish Gilroes
jewish-gilroes.org.uk/ancestor-search/
A genealogical and photographic record of the Jewish graves at Gilroes Cemetery, Leicester.

American Jewish Historical Society
ajhs.org/family-history
This page takes you straight to the body's list of collections.

Jewish Historical Society of England
jhse.org

Centre for Jewish History, genealogy guides
libguides.cjh.org/genealogyguides

The Miriam Weiner Routes to Roots Foundation
rtrfoundation.org/index.shtml

USC Shoah Foundation
sfi.usc.edu

Visual History Archive Online, Shoah Foundation
vhaonline.usc.edu/login.aspx

Association of Jewish Ex-Servicemen and Women
ajex.org.uk

Voices of the Holocaust
voices.iit.edu

Wiener Library
wienerlibrary.co.uk

Jewish Chronicle
thejc.com

Jewish Museum, London
jewishmuseum.org.uk

Manchester Jewish Museum
manchesterjewishmuseum.com

American Jewish Joint Distribution Committee
jdc.org

Free Jewish Databases, About.com
genealogy.about.com/od/jewish/tp/free_jewish.htm

See also: 2.12 Migration, 2.13 Overseas Research

2.20 Nonconformist Records

In 1559 the Act of Uniformity made the Church of England the established church. Though Catholics and Jews are sometimes referred to as nonconformists, in genealogical circles the term usually refers to non-Anglican Protestant denominations, the most common being Baptists, Methodists, Presbyterians and Quakers.

BMD Registers
bmdregisters.co.uk

Official TNA partner site that provides access to birth, baptism, marriage, death and burial data, taken from non-parish sources, relating to Methodists, Wesleyans, Baptists, Independents, Protestant Dissenters, Congregationalists, Presbyterians, Unitarians, Quakers, Dissenters and Russian Orthodox Church members. It's a pay-per-view system, but the same material is available via subscription with TheGenealogist.

My Methodist History
mymethodisthistory.org.uk

Community archive network that encourages users to share photos, stories, memories and research. There are also the sister sites My Primitive Methodist Ancestors (myprimitivemethodists.org.uk) and My Wesleyan Methodist Ancestors (mywesleyanmethodists.org.uk).

Quaker Archives, Leeds University Library
library.leeds.ac.uk/info/254/search_special_collections/148/summary_guide_to _the_quaker_archives/1

The Quaker Archives comprises the Carlton Hill collection (broadly covering Leeds, Bradford, Settle and Knaresborough) and the Clifford Street collection (York and Thirsk areas, plus Yorkshire-wide material). Through the beta version of the advanced search option you can isolate individual Quaker collections.

London Nonconformist registers 1694–1921, Ancestry
ancestry.co.uk/lma_nonconformist

Details nonconformist registers between 1694 and 1921 available through Ancestry's partnership with the London Metropolitan Archives. The site also hosts large collections of nonconformist/non-parochial registers of births, marriages and deaths in England and Wales.

Researching Nonconformists Guide, The National Archives
nationalarchives.gov.uk/records/research-guides/nonconformists.htm

Highlights the RG collections housed at Kew and details the different kinds of registers and records available online and offline – and what's searchable via the Discovery catalogue.

England Nonconformist Church Records, FamilySearch

familysearch.org/learn/wiki/en/England_Nonconformist_Church_Records

Exhaustive wiki page that introduces many of the most important subjects and sources for nonconformist research.

ScotlandsPeople

scotlandspeople.gov.uk

You can of course explore the OPRs via ScotlandsPeople; you can also read about the founding father of Protestant Reformation in Scotland, John Knox.

Methodist Westminster Central Hall, Historical Roll

methodist-central-hall.org.uk/index.php?option=com_content&view=category&id=31&Itemid=25

Contains the names of over 1 million people who donated a guinea to the Wesleyan Methodist Twentieth Century Fund between 1899 and 1904.

Quaker FHS

qfhs.co.uk

Includes pages explaining types of records available such as minute books, membership lists and BMD digests. This site has a useful county table to help you locate meeting records.

Methodist Archives and Research Centre

www.library.manchester.ac.uk/searchresources/guidetospecialcollections/methodist/

There's a PDF research guide plus a virtual library section where you can search various online texts.

Library of the Religious Society of Friends, and Quaker Centre

quaker.org.uk/library

The official library of the Religious Society of Friends, which now has a new online catalogue.

Conscientious Objectors, TNA guide

nationalarchives.gov.uk/records/looking-for-person/conscientiousobjectors.htm

As the refusal to bear arms is central to Quaker beliefs, many became conscientious objectors.

University of Nottingham Special Collections

nottingham.ac.uk/manuscriptsandspecialcollections/collectionsindepth/nonconformistchurches/collections.aspx

Lists nonconformist records held here.

England and Wales Nonconformist Marriages 1641–1852, Findmypast

search.findmypast.co.uk/search-world-records/england-and-wales-non-conformist-marriages

An example of Findmypast's nonconformist collections.

Chapels Society
chapelssociety.org.uk

Focuses on the history and architecture of nonconformist places of worship.

Baptist History and Heritage Society
baptisthistory.org/bhhs/

Wesley Historical Society
wesleyhistoricalsociety.org.uk

Dictionary of Methodism in Britain and Ireland
wesleyhistoricalsociety.org.uk/dmbi/

Presbyterian Historical Society of Ireland
presbyterianhistoryireland.com

See also: 1.4 Parish Registers, 2.18 Catholic, 2.19 Jewish

2.21 Photographs and Films

Daguerreotypes came into widespread use during the 1840s, and were gradually superseded by ambrotypes, ferreotypes, albumen prints and the *carte de visite*, before the age of portable cameras popularized low-cost photography. This chapter covers places to explore online image and film archives, and websites that can help you date your family photographs.

HistoryPin
historypin.org

Allows users to attach old photographs and memories to a global map. You can explore the images in a number of ways, and it's possible to view historic street

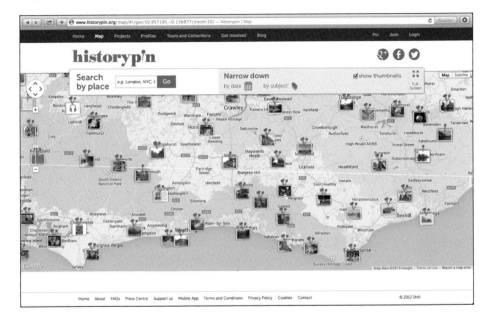

shots superimposed onto Google Street View. Currently, a flood of content related to the First World War is appearing, plus lots of UK archives, libraries and museums have HistoryPin feeds, where they upload their own collections.

BFI National Archive
bfi.org.uk/archive-collections

Details of BFI collections. There's Screenonline (screenonline.org.uk), an 'online encyclopaedia of British film and television', and Colonial Film (colonialfilm.org.uk), subtitled 'Moving images of the British Empire', with details of 6,000 films – 150 available to view online. You can also visit the YouTube channel at youtube.com/user/BFIfilms.

Victorian and Edwardian Photographs
rogerco.freeserve.co.uk

This simple website is based on a personal collection of *cartes de visite* and portrait postcards. It also includes useful galleries of dated images designed to help you put dates to your own photographs using changing Victorian fashions as your guide.

Flickr
flickr.com

Lots of archives, museums and libraries show off highlights from their image collections via Flickr. A couple of examples: Tyne and Wear Archives (flickr.com/photos/twm_news/) and the Public Record Office of Northern Ireland (flickr.com/photos/proni/).

Shetland Museum and Archives Photo Library
photos.shetland-museum.org.uk

Great example of a regional archive/museum photo library, with more than 65,000 images online documenting Shetland Life. You can use the index to narrow results by parish or subjects such as 'Wrecks' or 'Roll of Honour'.

English Heritage Archive
english-heritage.org.uk/professional/archives-and-collections/nmr/

Gateway to three photographic datasets: the archive's catalogue of over 1 million photographs and documents; Britain from Above (see below); and Images of England – 320,000 contemporary images of listed buildings.

Britain from Above
britainfromabove.org.uk

Explore 96,000 high-resolution aerial images taken between 1919 and 1953. You can search by place name, map or year, and register to provide information about the images.

European Film Gateway
europeanfilmgateway.eu

The EFG Portal gives you quick access to hundreds of thousands of films preserved in European film archives, including the likes of IWM and the Scottish Screen Archive.

Museum of London Picture Library

museumoflondonimages.com

Holds over 35,000 images illustrating 'the history of London and the life of its people from prehistoric times to the present'.

Portrait and Studio Photographers

earlyphotographers.org.uk/databases.html

Find information about professional photographers working in the UK in the nineteenth and early twentieth centuries. There's also a photo dating tool.

WDYTYA? Forum

whodoyouthinkyouaremagazine.com/forum/

Many users post photos on forums to help identify people, objects, buildings or time periods.

British Photographic History

britishphotohistory.ning.com

Useful hub for news and links for anything relating to photography and photographic heritage.

Royal Photographic Society

rps.org/publications/journal-archive

Online searchable journal archive of the Royal Photographic Society, which runs from 1853 to 2012.

Great War Forum

1914-1918.invisionzone.com

Post any photo of your military ancestor and ask for help with identifying cap badges, medals and insignia.

Early Photography

earlyphotography.co.uk

Cameras and equipment from the 'daguerreotype and wet-plate era'.

British Film Council

film.britishcouncil.org/resources/libraries-and-archives

Lists a few of the most important moving image archives in the UK.

People's Collection Wales

peoplescollectionwales.co.uk

Vast picture, image and artefact gallery drawn from Welsh archives and museums.

World of the Victorian Photographer

qvictoria.wordpress.com/victorian-photographers-ad-av/

Includes a database of UK photographers (1850–1900).

British Pathé
britishpathe.com
Explore newsreels, video and archive film footage and stills.

Wellcome Images
wellcomeimages.org
The Wellcome Trust online image library.

Yorkshire Film Archive
yorkshirefilmarchive.com

East Anglian Film Archive
eafa.org.uk

National Screen and Sound Archive of Wales
archif.com

National Media Museum
nationalmediamuseum.org.uk

Victoria and Albert Museum, Photography
vam.ac.uk/page/p/photography/

Press Photo History Project
pressphotohistory.com

Photography and the Archive Research Centre
photographyresearchcentre.co.uk

London Stereoscopic Company
londonstereo.com

Francis Frith
francisfrith.com

Screen South
screensouth.org

2.22 Londoners

The long-term partnership between Ancestry and the London Metropolitan Archives has meant vast genealogical collections are already digitally available, with more on the way. There's also a bewildering spread of specialist museum collections, borough archives and local studies libraries, meaning federated catalogues like TNA's Discovery and AIM25 come in very handy.

London Metropolitan Archives

lma.gov.uk

This is the kind of website where what you're looking for always seems to be one more click away. That said, it's better than it used to be and there's a dedicated catalogue at search.lma.gov.uk/opac_lma. The Family History page provides links to the Ancestry collections, and photographs, prints, maps and films can be explored via the Images and Film page. The Data and Websites page links to LMA material online elsewhere.

London Lives, 1690 to 1800

londonlives.org

The site carries the sub-head 'Crime, Poverty and Social Policy in the Metropolis', and contains fully searchable editions of 240,000 manuscripts from 8 archives and 15 datasets, giving access to 3.35 million names. Sources include court papers, criminal registers, coroners' inquests, Poor Law material and more.

London Collections, Ancestry

ancestry.co.uk/cs/uk/lma

Ancestry landing page for the LMA alliance, detailing many millions of parish registers, nonconformist registers, workhouse and Poor Law records, school registers, wills, electoral registers, poll books, marriage bonds and transportation papers that are appearing online.

AIM 25

www.aim25.ac.uk

Provides electronic access to collection-level descriptions of the archives of over 100 higher education institutions, learned societies, cultural organizations and livery companies within the Greater London area.

Collage

collage.cityoflondon.gov.uk/collage/app

Digitizing the London County Council Photograph Library of approximately 250,000 images from the 1860s to the 1980s. There are also other images and artefacts from both the LMA and the Guildhall Art Gallery.

Wandsworth Heritage Service

wandsworth.gov.uk/info/200064/local_history_and_heritage/888/heritage_service

Site includes free searches of the Wandsworth Cemeteries and Putney Vale Crematorium registries, plus an online catalogue; many of the images stored here are available to browse on Flickr.

Guildhall Library

cityoflondon.gov.uk/things-to-do/visiting-the-city/archives-and-city-history/guildhall-library/Pages/default.aspx

Another website that can leave you feeling thwarted. Collections held here include apprenticeship records and historic trade and telephone directories dating from 1736.

London's Screen Archives

londonsscreenarchives.org.uk

You can also access some collection highlights via the YouTube channel (youtube.com/user/LondonsScreenArchive/videos).

London's Pulse

wellcomelibrary.org/moh/

Part of the Wellcome Library's Digital Collections, here you can explore Medical Officer of Health Reports from the city between 1848 and 1972.

Hillingdon History Portal

hillingdon.gov.uk/history

Details of First World War commemorations, plus historic footage (via YouTube), local history, archival collections and an online catalogue.

DeceasedOnline

deceasedonline.com

Has more and more data from the so-called 'Magnificent Seven' London cemeteries.

London Registers

www.parishregister.com

Commercial site offering transcribed parish data for London, particularly the Docklands.

Bomb Sight

bombsight.org

Explore the bomb census of the London Blitz from October 1940 to June 1941.

Proceedings of the Old Bailey

www.oldbaileyonline.org

The proceedings from London's Central Criminal Court between 1674 and 1913.

Abney Park Cemetery Trust

abneypark.org

Includes a database of names of those buried at the cemetery.

Thames Pilot

www.thamespilot.org.uk

Useful source for images relating to the river.

Hackney Archives

hackney.gov.uk/ca-archives

There's an online catalogue and you can explore historic images.

Highgate Cemetery

highgatecemetery.org

Tower Hamlets Archives
towerhamlets.gov.uk/lgsl/1001-1050/1034_local_history__archives.aspx

London Museums of Health and Medicine
medicalmuseums.org/home/

Barking and Dagenham Archives and Local Studies Centre
www.lbbd.gov.uk/services/archives-and-local-studies-centre/

Newham Archives and Local Studies Library
www.newham.gov.uk/Pages/ServiceChild/Newham-Archives-and-Local-Studies-Library.aspx

Museum of London / Museum of London Docklands
museumoflondon.org.uk
museumindocklands.org.uk

Bishopsgate Institute Library
www.bishopsgate.org.uk

Richmond Burial Registers database
richmond.gov.uk/cemeteries

Barnes and Mortlake History Society
barnes-history.org.uk

London Topographical Society
topsoc.org

Teddington Society
teddingtonsociety.org.uk

Brent Archives
www.brent.gov.uk/archive

Ealing Local History Centre
www.ealing.gov.uk/info/200461/local_history_centre

Hammersmith and Fulham Archives
www.lbhf.gov.uk/Directory/Leisure_and_Culture/Libraries/Archives/

Harrow Local History Centre
www.harrow.gov.uk/info/200070/museums_and_galleries/183/harrow_local_history_centre

Hounslow Archives
www.hounslow.info/libraries/local-history-archives/family-history/

Richmond Local Studies
richmond.gov.uk/local_studies_collection

London Westminster and Middlesex FHS
lwmfhs.org.uk

East of London FHS
eolfhs.org.uk

West Middlesex FHS
west-middlesex-fhs.org.uk

See also: 5.1 Resources by Region

2.23 Maps

A huge range of map-based online projects have launched in recent years, led by companies such as klokantech.com and crowdsourcing drives like HistoryPin. There are also some dated – but still very useful – sites that allow you to explore the same location backwards and forwards in time.

OldMapsOnline
oldmapsonline.org

Brings together 'geo-referenced map metadata' from historic maps held at the likes of the British Library, Bodleian Library, National Library of Scotland, A Vision of Britain Through Time (website: see below), and many more overseas repositories. You can click Collections to find more detailed descriptions of the kinds of historic maps preserved by the partner institutions.

ScotlandsPlaces
scotlandsplaces.gov.uk

Wonderful resource, aimed at investigating Scotland's physical heritage, which allows users to search archival collections by geographic location. From the homepage you can either type in a place/coordinate, or use the site's own map to refine your search. The website draws on material from several important national collections, including maps and plans of settlements and buildings.

Vision of Britain
visionofbritain.org.uk

Not as cutting-edge as it once seemed, this is nevertheless a good place to start searching through maps of an area. Simply type your postcode or place name into the search box, and an historic map of the area appears. You can zoom in to individual buildings, explore surroundings, and choose various other maps of the area going back to 1805.

Cynefin: A Sense of Place
cynefin.archiveswales.org.uk

Most recent and best-looking example of several tithe map digitization projects (more are listed below). This is an HLF/Archives Wales project which grants us

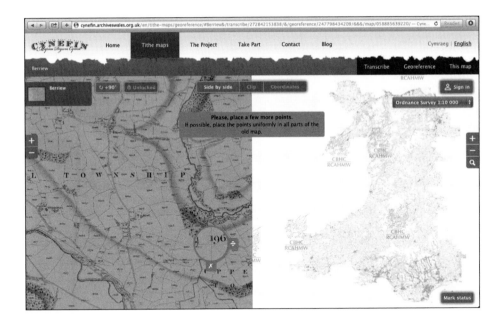

access to 1,200 sheets of Welsh tithe maps online – that's roughly 95 per cent of the country. The accompanying apportionment documents are currently being transcribed by volunteers.

National Library of Scotland
maps.nls.uk/

Access high-resolution zoomable images of over 91,000 maps of Scotland and beyond. These are free-to-view high-quality scans and include marine charts, military maps, estate maps, various town plans and views from 1580 to 1919, as well as Ordnance Survey maps. In 2014 these were joined by detailed First World War trench maps (maps.nls.uk/ww1/trenches).

British History Online
british-history.ac.uk/catalogue/maps

Hosts historic maps of London from before 1800 and maps from the nineteenth-century series of the Ordnance Survey, including the complete 1:10,560 series and selected areas of the 1:2,500 series.

Griffith's Valuation
askaboutireland.ie/griffith-valuation/index.xml

The first full-scale valuation of property in Ireland was overseen by Dublin geologist Richard Griffith between 1847 and 1864. Here you can find copies of the original documents and see the original valuation maps.

Norfolk E-Maps

historic-maps.norfolk.gov.uk

View historical maps alongside historical aerial survey data and modern day Ordnance Survey maps. There are nearly 700 tithe maps here covering about 85 per cent of the county.

MAPCO

mapco.net

Provides access to high-quality scans of rare and beautiful antique maps and views. The site displays a variety of highly collectable eighteenth- and nineteenth-century maps and plans of London and the British Isles.

Addressing History

addressinghistory.edina.ac.uk

Combines data from digitized historical Scottish post office directories with historical maps; currently focuses on Edinburgh, Glasgow and Aberdeen.

West Yorkshire Tithe Map Project

tracksintime.wyjs.org.uk

Free access to historic tithe maps which you can mount in twin browsers to compare the changing landscape through time.

Maps for Family and Local History Guide, The National Archives

nationalarchives.gov.uk/maps/maps-family-local-history.htm

TNA guidance with lots of useful links. Details of almost 12,000 tithe maps held here are now searchable through Discovery.

Your Old Books and Maps

youroldbooksandmaps.co.uk

Republishes rare books and maps on disc and/or PDF download, including maps from all over the UK.

Map History

maphistory.info

Maintained by respected authority Tony Campbell, former map librarian of the British Library.

Building History

buildinghistory.org/maps.shtml

Outline history of mapping in the British Isles, with lots of hyperlinks to online maps and charts.

Bomb Sight

bombsight.org

Explore this digital bomb census of the London Blitz overlaid on a modern map.

National Library of Wales
llgc.org.uk/collections/digital-gallery/maps0/
Access digital copies of the vast collection of maps held here.

E-mapping Victorian Cheshire: Cheshire Tithe Maps
maps.cheshire.gov.uk/tithemaps/
Home to almost 500 Cheshire tithe maps plus apportionments.

David Rumsey Map Collection Database
davidrumsey.com
This historical map collection has over 55,000 maps and images online.

Charting the Nation
www.chartingthenation.lib.ed.ac.uk
Maps of Scotland and associated archives 1550–1740.

National Collection of Tithes, TheGenealogist
thegenealogist.co.uk/featuredarticles/2014/the-national-collection-of-tithe-records-134/
Access to 11 million tithe records.

Dorset Coast Digital Archive
dcda.org.uk

Bodleian Library's Map Room
www.bodleian.ox.ac.uk/maps

British Library, Maps
bl.uk/onlinegallery/onlineex/maps/

Ordnance Survey
ordnancesurvey.co.uk

Old Maps
old-maps.co.uk

2.24 Estate Records

Estate records and family papers can be time-consuming and confusing, without offering any guarantee of results. However, it's always worth checking what catalogues and finding aids exist, as these collections can not only tell you a great deal about the parent family or landowner, but also may represent your best chance of finding references to individuals who lived or worked on the estate.

Estate and Manorial records, The National Archives
nationalarchives.gov.uk/records/looking-for-place/landedestates.htm
Via the 'Looking for a Place?' signposts, you can find this guide to researching landed estates (although the records online section isn't comprehensive). You can

search for estate papers held here via Discovery, which also details estate collections held externally and now includes the Manorial Documents Register of England and Wales.

Sutherland Collection
www.sutherlandcollection.org.uk

Fully indexed website built around the archive created by the Leveson-Gower family, the Marquesses of Stafford and the Dukes of Sutherland, which contains many thousands of names, including: employees, tenants, shopkeepers and suppliers, savers in the Trentham Savings Bank, and workers on the building of Trentham Hall.

Lives and Livelihoods in Conisbrough Manor
hrionline.ac.uk/conisbrough/

Explore one of the most important royal manors of Yorkshire through court rolls that give an account of the working lives and relationships of its inhabitants.

Estate Records Guide, National Records of Scotland
nrscotland.gov.uk/research/guides/estate-records

This guide covers locating landowners, and some types of records such as rent rolls, leases (tacks), household accounts and documents about estate buildings.

Images of England, English Heritage
www.imagesofengland.org.uk

Photographic library of England's listed buildings, recorded at the turn of the twenty-first century: contains more than 300,000 images.

Nottingham University Collections

nottingham.ac.uk/ManuscriptsandSpecialCollections/CollectionsInDepth/Family/Introduction.aspx

The Family and Estate Collections represent some of the most important Nottinghamshire landowning families. This page lists the families with links to catalogue information.

Arley Hall Archives 1750–90

arleyhallarchives.co.uk

Illuminates life and work in a country house in Cheshire in the late eighteenth century.

University of Hull Archives

hull.ac.uk/arc/collection/landedfamilyandestatepapers/index.html

Family and estate collections with some manorial records that date back to 1317.

Estate Records Guide, Public Record Office of Northern Ireland

www.proni.gov.uk/your_family_tree_series_-_08_-_landed_estate_records.pdf

Downloadable landed estates research guide.

National Trust Collections

nationaltrustcollections.org.uk

Explore items from more than 200 National Trust property collections.

Historic Houses Association

hha.org.uk

BuildingHistory

buildinghistory.org

Foundation for Medieval Genealogy

fmg.ac/FMG/Links.htm

The Harleian Society

harleian.org.uk

See also: 2.2 Probate and Wills, 2.3 Taxation, 2.25 Seventeenth- and Eighteenth-Century Sources, 5.4 Medieval Ancestors, 5.5 Heraldry, 5.6 Nobility and Gentry

2.25 Seventeenth- and Eighteenth-Century Sources

As a general rule the further back in time your research takes you, the harder your task becomes. It's also true that in general the richer your family were, the more substantial the paper trail is likely to be. So if you are venturing back to before the census and civil registration, potential sources include parish, tax, electoral and court records.

ConnectedHistories

connectedhistories.org

Allows you to search data from the likes of London Lives 1690–1800, British History Online, British Newspapers 1600–1900, Lane's Masonic Records and more. Some material here requires a subscription, but there's lots that is entirely free and the homepage's date slider means you can explore the past by blocks of twenty-five years.

Protestation Returns, Parliamentary Archives

www.parliament.uk/business/publications/parliamentary-archives/archives-highlights/familyhistory/sources/protestations/

By order of the House of Commons, all adult men were asked to swear an oath of allegiance to the Protestant religion. These Protestation Returns are described as the closest we have to a census from 1642. You can also find out more about Returns of Roman Catholics between 1680 and 1781.

Collection List, FamilySearch

familysearch.org/search/collection/list

This address is a useful shortcut to a simple list of published collections on FamilySearch. You can then narrow by various filters, including fifty-year date ranges, and explore all material covering the seventeenth and eighteenth centuries.

Old Bailey Online
www.oldbaileyonline.org

Free access to the fully searchable edition of Proceedings of the Old Bailey, 1674–1913, offering an unrivalled window onto crime and punishment in the seventeenth and eighteenth centuries.

E 179 Database, The National Archives
apps.nationalarchives.gov.uk/e179/

'Particulars of account and other records relating to lay and clerical taxation.' You can search the database by place, grant of taxation, date or type of document.

Hearth Tax Online
hearthtax.org.uk

Providing data from records of the hearth tax, introduced in England and Wales by the government of Charles II in 1662.

British Newspaper Archive
britishnewspaperarchive.co.uk

The news hub also has a useful date-range tool, meaning you can quickly explore titles available from specific periods.

TheGenealogist
thegenealogist.co.uk

Eighteenth-century material includes 58,000 militia muster records from England and Wales dating from the 1780s.

Old Maps Online
project.oldmapsonline.org/about

Access to map collections from the likes of the British Library and the National Library of Scotland.

Taxation Research Guide, National Archives of Scotland
nas.gov.uk/guides/taxation.asp

Also provides links to tax sources available through Scotland's Places (scotlandsplaces.gov.uk).

Findmypast
findmypast.co.uk

Has lots of material from the era including vast probate collections previously available through nationalwillsindex.com.

Legacies of British Slave-Ownership
ucl.ac.uk/lbs

Relates to the apprenticeship and compensation systems set up following the abolition of slavery.

The National Archives, A–Z Research Guides

nationalarchives.gov.uk/records/atoz/

From here you can browse multiple TNA guides relevant to the period.

Seventeenth/Eighteenth-Century sources, BBC Family History

bbc.co.uk/history/familyhistory/next_steps/adv_07_17_and_18_01.shtml

Excellent guide by Society of Genealogists' Else Churchill.

London Land Tax Records, 1692–1932, Ancestry

search.ancestry.co.uk/search/db.aspx?dbid=2170

Just one of several collections available via Ancestry.

Historical Directories

leicester.contentdm.oclc.org/cdm/landingpage/collection/p16445coll4

Has some directories dating back to 1750.

English Civil War, Cyndi's List

cyndislist.com/uk/military/historical/english-civil-war/

Cromwell 400

www.lib.cam.ac.uk/exhibitions/Cromwell/

See also: 1.4 Parish Registers, 2.2 Probate and Wills, 2.3 Taxation, 2.6 Court Records, 2.24 Estate Records, 2.26 Slavery, 3.4 Militia Men, 3.5 Napoleonic Wars, 5.4 Medieval Ancestors, 5.5 Heraldry

2.26 Slavery

While there are relatively few records of individual slaves, there is a lot of online information about voyages, vessels, crews and the men and women who profited from slavery, plus the abolition movements in Britain, Europe and America.

Legacies of British Slave-Ownership

ucl.ac.uk/lbs

When Parliament abolished slavery in the British Caribbean, Mauritius and the Cape, an apprenticeship scheme was introduced for freed individuals, and compensation was paid to former owners. The resulting records form the core of this UCL database, where you can find owners and see both how much they were awarded and the number of slaves at each property. There's a project blog (lbsatucl.wordpress.com) which includes interesting case studies.

Trans-Atlantic Slave Trade Database

slavevoyages.org

Those who profited from slaves tended to keep careful records and this website hosts a database of more than 35,000 slave-trading voyages, detailing owners, captains and crew. There's also a database of 91,491 Africans taken from captured slave ships or from African trading sites, giving name, age, gender, origin, country, and places of embarkation/disembarkation.

International Slavery Museum
liverpoolmuseums.org.uk/ism/

Information on the trade triangle: from European ports towards Africa's west coast; the voyage across the Atlantic known as the Middle Passage; and the return to Europe with goods produced by slave labour. You can also read two very different accounts of life on board a slave ship – from slave trader John Newton and former slave Olaudah Equiano.

Black Presence in Britain
blackpresence.co.uk

Under Black History > Slavery there are articles and material relating to the subject, plus links to free e-book editions of slave narratives such as *The History of Mary Prince, a West Indian Slave*. This was the first account of the life of a black woman to be published in England, and it had a galvanizing effect on the anti-slavery movement.

Understanding Slavery Initiative
understandingslavery.com

Image-rich project that draws on collections from six UK museums – including the International Slavery Museum and the National Maritime Museum. Galleries explore treatment of slaves, the economics of slavery, life on plantations and more.

Abolition of Slavery, The National Archives
nationalarchives.gov.uk/slavery/

View samples of slave ship logs and abolitionists' wills, and explore TNA guides and external sources such as slave registers (1812–34) from Ancestry; most registers have indexes to slave owners and estates, and give the name of the parish or district where they lived.

Parliament and the British Slave Trade
www.parliament.uk/slavetrade   archives.gov/research/alic/reference/state-archives.html

Explore Parliament's relationship with both transatlantic slavery and the public campaign against it. There's material about trade routes, members of London's black community, abolitionists and petitions, and House of Commons debates.

Recovered Histories
recoveredhistories.org

Digitized eighteenth- and nineteenth-century literature on the transatlantic slave trade – including narratives from 'the enslaved, enslavers, slave ship surgeons, abolitionists, parliamentarians, clergy, planters and rebels'.

Slavery, Abolition and Emancipation
brycchancarey.com/slavery/index.htm

Has a timeline, biographies of British abolitionists – including Ignatius Sancho, the first known African to vote in a British election – and extracts from the writings of freed slave Olaudah Equiano.

Researching Slavery, Ancestry
ancestry.co.uk/wiki/index.php?title=Researching_Slavery

Ancestry Wiki article on the subject. You can also search TNA Slave Registers of former British Colonial Dependencies (1813–34) on the Ancestry site.

Wilberforce Institute for the Study of Slavery and Emancipation
www2.hull.ac.uk/fass/wise/about_us.aspx

Contains details of collections held here, plus information about the Global Slavery Index (globalslaveryindex.org).

Centre for the Study of International Slavery, University of Liverpool
liv.ac.uk/csis/

Includes the Black Atlantic Resource at: liv.ac.uk/black-atlantic/.

Mémoire St Barth
memoirestbarth.com/EN/

Explores the impact of slavery on Saint-Barthélemy, an island of the Lesser Antilles.

Discovering Bristol, Slavery
discoveringbristol.org.uk/slavery/

Find out about Bristol's role in the transatlantic slave trade.

London, Sugar and Slavery, Museum of London
archive.museumoflondon.org.uk/LSS/

Mills Plantation Archive, Museum of London
museumoflondon.org.uk/collections-research/about-collections/mills-plantation-archive/

The Wreck of the Henrietta Marie
melfisher.org/henriettamarie.htm

My Slave Ancestors
myslaveancestors.com

Slave Genealogy
slavegenealogy.com

Breaking the Silence
old.antislavery.org/breakingthesilence/

Anti-Slavery International

antislavery.org

UNESCO's Slave Route

unesco.org/new/en/culture/themes/dialogue/the-slave-route

*See also: 2.11 Newspapers, 2.12 Migration, 2.13 Overseas Research, 2.25 Seventeenth-
and Eighteenth-Century Sources*

2.27 Sports and Pastimes

Britain's class system had a huge impact on global sport. The professional–
amateur divide would shape cricket, football, tennis, athletics, and split rugby in
two. Finding evidence of your own ancestor's sporting achievements may be
confined to family archives or school magazines, but if they were talented
enough to play for club or country, there are museums, archives and sites where
you can find out more.

National Football Museum

nationalfootballmuseum.com/collections/family-history/

Family history advice from the National Football Museum in Manchester.
Although the text here has remained unchanged for some time, they are still
working to digitize FA and Football League records.

British Newspaper Archive

britishnewspaperarchive.co.uk

This ever-expanding commercial database has coverage of all sports, from major
internationals matches, to the local and school results often featured in local
newspapers. Plus it has specialist titles such as the *Sports Argus* (1914–18).

Olympic Movement

olympic.org/olympic-games

Read facts and figures from all past Olympic Games from the official website of
the Olympic Movement. You can also find out about the Olympic Museum and
the Olympic Studies Centre, both of which are in Switzerland.

British Pathé

britishpathe.com/gallery/1908-london-olympics-photos

View footage and photos taken from all kinds of sporting events. This page takes
you to a modest gallery relating to the rather dreary-looking London Games of
1908.

Cric Info

espncricinfo.com

Via the Archive section you can search the *Wisden* back catalogue to 1864, with
lots of reproduced essays and obituaries.

Cricket Archive
cricketarchive.co.uk
Home to a growing database of 530,000+ full and partial scorecards, and details of 531,000+ players.

Association of Cricket Statisticians and Historians
acscricket.com
Now hosts the Online Cricket Records section – covering first-class cricket, Test cricket, List A and Twenty20.

The Fosters of Malvern
thefostersofmalvern.co.uk
The sporting achievements of seven members of the same family.

Rugby League Heritage
www.rugbyleaguecares.org/heritage

Football Club History Database
fchd.info

Soccer Data
soccerdata.co.uk

Association of Football Statisticians
11v11.co.uk

Rugby Football History
rugbyfootballhistory.com

Talk Rugby Union
talkrugbyunion.co.uk

Bicycle Racing
theracingbicycle.com

British Golf Museum
britishgolfmuseum.co.uk

Wimbledon Heritage
wimbledon.com/heritage

Scottish Football Museum, Hampden Park
scottishfootballmuseum.org.uk

Lord's
lords.org/history/mcc-museum-library-and-collections/mcc-museum/

Elizabethan Sports
www.elizabethan-era.org.uk/elizabethan-sports.htm

Section 3

MILITARY AND CONFLICT

3.1 Army

These are the most useful websites for the researching of any individual who served with the army. They include general history websites, plus free and subscription-based collections and finding aids. Remember to check chapters dedicated to specific conflicts such as the First World War and the Boer War.

Army Guides, The National Archives

nationalarchives.gov.uk

Follow the 'Looking for a Person?' signposts to find army personnel research guides – these are divided by date ranges (such as soldiers before and after 1913) and subjects (such as Militia, Home Guard or Volunteers and Territorials). There's also Medals and Honours, or you can explore digitized online sources via Catalogues and Online Records (nationalarchives.gov.uk/records/catalogues-and-online-records.htm).

Commonwealth War Graves Commission

cwgc.org

Searchable database of the 1,700,000 service personnel who died during the two world wars, plus a further 67,000 Commonwealth civilians who died as a result of enemy actions during the Second World War. You can search by name, date, war, rank, regiment or awards. Via Find a Cemetery you can also find information, images and plans of individual cemeteries and memorials, then search among names of the individuals commemorated.

The Long, Long Trail

1914-1918.net

Chris Baker's exhaustive history of the British army in the First World War is aimed at family historians and enthusiasts. Its uncluttered design masks the vast amount of material held here, which is organized into five main sections: Regiments, Formations, Battles, Army Life and Regulations. Beginners should start with the Researching a Soldier page.

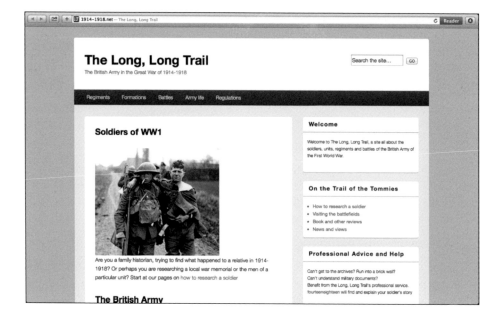

The Sandhurst Collection

archive.sandhurstcollection.co.uk

The Royal Military Academy's archives go back to the eighteenth century, and here you can search cadet/staff registers, which contain details of almost every officer cadet who attended the Royal Military Academy Woolwich and the Royal Military College Sandhurst; the register records each cadet's name, age, date of entry, commissioning date and corps or regiment joined. Searches are free, downloading an image costs £2.99.

Military Collections, Ancestry

ancestry.co.uk/military

Here you can access army service records (1914–20), which reveal rank, regiment, where served, medals received and personal details, pension records, campaign medals (1793–1949) and indexes to recommendations for honours and awards (1935–90). The top right 'All our military collections' box allows you to narrow collections by conflict.

Armed Forces and Conflict, Findmypast

search.findmypast.co.uk/search-united-kingdom-records-in-military-armed-forces-and-conflict

This is the 'all collections' search page for FMP's military databases. You can also try their First World War launch page (findmypast.co.uk/ww1), which details key sources such as British army service records. Boasts over 12.5 million British records relating to military service, with records of servicemen from both world wars, the Anglo-Boer, Korean, Spanish Civil and Napoleonic Wars. There are army lists, draft records, pension records, and lists of awards and decorations.

Royal Army Medical Corps, Wellcome Library

wellcomelibrary.org/collections/digital-collections/royal-army-medical-corps/

Digitized archive covering more than 150 years of military medicine and wartime experiences of the Royal Army Medical Corps. It includes more than 130,000 digitized pages of correspondence, reports, personal field diaries, memoirs, photographs and memorabilia from the Army Medical Services Museum.

Anglo-Afghan War

garenewing.co.uk/angloafghanwar/

History of the Second Anglo-Afghan War (1878–1880) and the disastrous march from Kabul to Kandahar. There's also an excellent links page leading to sites dedicated to other Victorian conflicts.

British Army War Diaries 1914–22, The National Archives

nationalarchives.gov.uk/records/war-diaries-ww1.htm

Selected collection of digitized war diaries of units in the British army from TNA record series WO 95. This is one of several digitized TNA collections available through the Discovery catalogue.

Australian War Memorial

awm.gov.au

Includes all kinds of material relating to the Australian experience of war, including centenary digitization project ANZAC Connections, and details of personnel serving in pre-First World War conflicts.

National Army Museum

national-army-museum.ac.uk

The place to explore army history from 1485 to the present. The site has greatly improved in recent years, and you can view sample documents, photographs and prints via the Online Collection.

Soldiers' Wills, ScotlandsPeople

scotlandspeople.gov.uk

Towards the base of the left-hand menu you'll find a Soldiers' Wills database. Most of these are for rank-and-file soldiers and the majority date from the First World War.

Operation War Diary

operationwardiary.org

Crowdsourcing project seeking to unlock the hidden stories contained within 1.5 million pages of First World War unit war diaries.

Army Family History, Imperial War Museum

iwm.org.uk/collections-research/tracing-your-family-history/tracing-your-army-history

Detailed guide to tracing your army ancestors which covers service, casualty and medal records, regimental histories and useful links.

Army Museums Ogilby Trust
armymuseums.org.uk/ancestor.htm

Register of museums, plus this general introduction to researching army ancestors.

The Ministry of Defence
www.gov.uk/requests-for-personal-data-and-service-records

Holds records relating to soldiers who served after 1920 (other ranks) and 1922 (officers).

Forces War Records
forces-war-records.co.uk

Specialist subscription site which has all kinds of army material that you can explore by conflict/era.

Military Archives
militaryarchives.ie

Records of Ireland's Department of Defence, the Defence Forces and the Army Pensions Board.

Women's Army Auxiliary Corps Service Records 1917–20, The National Archives
nationalarchives.gov.uk/records/womens-army-auxiliary-corps.htm

TNA-held service records of more than 7,000 women who joined the WAAC.

British Army
army.mod.uk

Click British Army Structure to find out more about individual regiments and their history.

The Gazette
www.thegazette.co.uk

Search and browse military awards from MiDs to the Victoria Cross.

British Army Medal Index Cards, The National Archives
nationalarchives.gov.uk/records/medal-index-cards-ww1.htm

British army medal index cards (1914–20).

Royal Engineers Museum, Library and Archive
re-museum.co.uk

Army Children Archive
archhistory.co.uk

Army Medical Services Museum
ams-museum.org.uk/museum/

See also: 3.4 Militia Men, 3.5 Napoleonic Wars, 3.6 Victorian Wars, 3.7 Boer Wars, 3.8 First World War, 3.9 Second World War, 3.10 POWs, 3.12 Medals, 3.13 War Graves

3.2 Navy

The dominance of the Senior Service was instrumental in establishing and maintaining the British Empire. And online the subject is well served: from sites that focus on the exploits of heroic commanders, to the tactics employed in bloody naval battles, to the mass digitizing of key maritime sources.

Navy Collections, The National Archives

nationalarchives.gov.uk/records/navy.htm

At the time of writing there were fourteen research guides focusing on navy personnel, with yet more that focused on related topics such as Royal Marines, the Royal Naval Air Service and Merchant Seaman. This page lists some of the most popular digitized collections that are already available to search and view, print or download (for a fee), including more than 600,000 Royal Navy ratings' service records (1853–1923) and Royal Marines' service records (1842–1925).

Navy Lists, Archive.org

archive.org/details/nlsnavylists

A useful free resource available via archive.org is the collection of official British Navy Lists – these particular volumes have been scanned from the National Library of Scotland, with the earliest dating from 1819 and many dating from the Second World War. You can either explore volumes through your browser or download in various formats. Information included varies but will often include officers' dates of seniority, prizes, naval medals and ships/battles.

Commonwealth War Graves Commission, Find a Cemetery

www.cwgc.org/find-a-cemetery.aspx

Following the First World War the Admiralty commissioned three memorials for casualties with no known grave. These were located at their manning ports – Portsmouth, Plymouth and Chatham. With the Find a Cemetery tool you can isolate names from individual memorials like these – the Portsmouth Naval Memorial, for example, records 24,588 individuals, revealing name, age, rank and where the person is recorded on the memorial.

Naval Service Records, Findmypast

search.findmypast.co.uk/search-united-kingdom-records-in-military-armed-forces-and-conflict

Findmypast released 500,000 British Royal Navy and Marine Service records (1899–1919) in April 2014. This is one of several sources available through its ongoing partnership with TNA. Others include Royal Naval Division Service Records (1914–20) and the Royal Navy Officers Medal Roll (1914–20).

National Maritime Museum

collections.rmg.co.uk

The Museum's Collections page, where you can read about and search the Archive/Library catalogue. The site also has lots of permanent and temporary exhibitions – recent examples include the Forgotten Fighters gallery which focuses on lesser-known stories of the First World War.

Trafalgar Ancestors, The National Archives

apps.nationalarchives.gov.uk/trafalgarancestors/

Alongside research guides to officers and ratings of the era, you can search this TNA database of more than 18,000 individuals who fought in the Battle of Trafalgar – along with service histories/biographical details.

Naval History.net

naval-history.net

This vast site is produced and maintained by a team of specialist contributors, and has sections on RN operations, honours/awards, battles, dispatches and more. These include 350,000 pages of transcribed log books from the First World War.

Officer and Rating Service Records, Ancestry

ancestry.co.uk/cs/uk/military

Important collections on Ancestry include Naval Medal and Award Rolls (1793–1972) and Naval Officer and Rating Service Records (1802–1919). The latter includes musters and pay registers.

Forces War Records

forces-war-records.co.uk

Has data relating to the Royal Naval College in Dartmouth, and the Royal Marines' and Royal Navy officers' campaign medal rolls (1914–20), and a database of Royal Navy/Royal Marines recipients of the 1914 Star Medal.

Age of Nelson

ageofnelson.org

Hosts two useful databases – Royal Navy officers in the French Revolutionary and Napoleonic wars (1793–1815), and the seamen and marines who fought at the Battle of Trafalgar in 1805.

World War 1 Naval Combat

worldwar1.co.uk

Has sections focusing on the Battle of Heligoland Bight, the loss of HMS *Audacious*, the battles of Dogger Bank and Jutland, and the Scapa Flow scuttling.

Battle of Jutland, Imperial War Museum

iwm.org.uk/history/the-battle-of-jutland

IWM page dedicated to this 'confused and bloody action' – the major naval battle of the First World War.

Royal Navy Research Archives

royalnavyresearcharchive.org.uk

A virtual museum dedicated to RN ships, bases, units and personnel – mainly from the First World War onwards.

Books, Boxes and Boats

maritimearchives.co.uk

Brings together a wide variety of websites and databases – such as online copies of Lloyd's Register and the Mercantile Navy List.

Ships Pictures
shipspictures.co.uk

Specialist hub which, at time of writing, boasted some 10,397 warships, 81 army ships, 91 merchant ships and 15 tall ships.

HMS Victory
hms-victory.com

Official website for Nelson's flagship which gives background detail about the lives of members of the Georgian navy.

Empire and Sea Power, BBC History
www.bbc.co.uk/history/british/empire_seapower/

Currently being overhauled, but still a readable introduction to Britain's maritime heritage.

Old Weather
oldweather.org

Project to chart historic weather patterns recorded in captains' logs.

Maritime Quest
maritimequest.com

'A quest for the photographic history of the world's ships.'

Submarines of the Great War
dropbears.com/w/ww1subs/

Fascinating stories of early submarine warfare.

Navy Photos
navyphotos.co.uk

Information and images about specific vessels.

Battle of Jutland
battle-of-jutland.com

Naval Warships, Submarines and Watercraft
militaryfactory.com/ships/index.asp

Navy Records Society
navyrecordsonline.co.uk

Portsmouth Historic Dockyard
historicdockyard.co.uk

See also: 3.5 Napoleonic Wars, 3.6 Victorian Wars, 3.8 First World War, 3.9 Second World War, 3.10 POWs, 3.12 Medals, 3.13 War Graves, 4.5 Merchant Navy

3.3 Royal Air Force

Significant anniversaries in the history of the RAF have seen more and more material pour online in recent years. The next milestone falls in 2018: 100 years since the formation of the Royal Air Force from its predecessors the Royal Flying Corps and Royal Naval Air Service.

RAF Museum StoryVault
rafmuseumstoryvault.org.uk

RAF's StoryVault captures stories of ordinary servicemen and servicewomen; plus there are digitized archives of conflict casualty cards, the 1918 muster roll and the 1918 Air Force List. You can find out more about the RAF Museums at Cosford and London via rafmuseum.org.uk. The collections page has photographs, and information about medals and uniforms; you can also buy facsimile reprints of various historic documents.

RAF Research Guide, The National Archives
nationalarchives.gov.uk / records / research-guides / raf-rfc-rnas.htm

This page focuses on RAF personnel, but there are also related guides to squadrons, RFC officers / airmen, and RNAS officers / ratings. Online records currently available include combat reports (1939–45), RAF officers' service records (1918 – 19) and WRAF service records (1918–20).

Royal Air Force Officers' Service Records, The National Archives
nationalarchives.gov.uk / records / raf-officers-ww1.htm

This is one of the most important RAF datasets already available online via TNA: the service records of officers who served during the First World War. This collection, in series AIR 76, consists of the records of over 99,000 men; these records date from the inception of the RAF in April 1918. You can search for free, and individual image downloads currently cost £3.30.

RAF Records, Findmypast

findmypast.co.uk/content/RAF_Records

Findmypast now offers access to TNA's AIR 76 (Officers' service records, 1912–20) and AIR 79 (Airmen's records, 1912–39). Plus they have the RAF Muster Roll from April 1918, which recorded every serviceman enlisted when it was created, and which contains references to more than 181,000 men, listed by service number.

Battle of Britain Memorial

battleofbritainmemorial.org

The focus of events surrounding the seventy-fifth anniversary of the Battle of Britain in 2015. You can also see photographs of the Capel-le-Ferne National Memorial and the Battle of Britain Memorial Wall, which records the names of all recipients of the Battle of Britain Clasp.

RAF Museum Navigator

navigator.rafmuseum.org

Dedicated catalogue and gallery space for the RAF Museum's collections. You can also view image highlights via Flickr (flickr.com/photos/royalairforcemuseum/).

Air Historical Branch, RAF

raf.mod.uk/ahb/recordsofservice/

The official Air Historical Branch information page which tells you more about records of service. There are also pages on POWs, burials and memorials.

Forces War Records

forces-war-records.co.uk

Datasets include RAF Formations List 1918, Fighter Command Losses 1940 and Aviators Certificates 1905–26.

Royal Flying Corps 1914–18

airwar1.org.uk

History of the Royal Flying Corps and its aircraft. Click on A Pilot's War to read stories of individual pilots and squadrons.

Bomber History

bomberhistory.co.uk

Has sections telling the stories of 49 Squadron, plus accounts of specific raids and air attacks on British soil.

Fleet Air Arm Archive

fleetairarmarchive.net

Has a Debt of Honour Register, POW database and biographies of decorated officers.

Western Front Association
westernfrontassociation.com
Under Naval and Air War you'll find sections on aircraft, aces and combat.

History of RAF
rafweb.org
Includes histories of units and stations, plus a lot of links.

Bomber Command
rafbombercommand.com
History of RAF bomber aircrews, airmen and airwomen during the Second World War.

Dambusters Blog
dambustersblog.com
Has biographical details of individual members of the raid.

Bomber Crew
bombercrew.com
Dated but nonetheless interesting website.

Requests for Service Records
www.gov.uk/requests-for-personal-data-and-service-records
Official Government guide to requesting more recent service records.

Cross and Cockade International
www.crossandcockade.com
First World War aviation historical society.

Air Force Cross, Wikipedia
en.wikipedia.org/wiki/Air_Force_Cross_(United_Kingdom)
Includes lots of links to descriptions and histories of other military decorations.

Tracing Your RFC/RAF Family History, IWM
iwm.org.uk/collections-and-research/tracing-your-family-history/royal-flying-corps-and-royal-air-force-family

Royal Air Force Ex-POW Association
rafinfo.org.uk/rafexpow/

Air Force POWs, RAF Commands
rafcommands.com/old-site/air-force-pows/

Unit Histories
unithistories.com

Museum of Army Flying
armyflying.com

RAF Casualties 1935–50, Family Relatives
familyrelatives.com/search/search_wwiiairforce.php

Royal Air Forces Association
rafa.org.uk

FlyPast
flypast.com

See also: 3.8 First World War, 3.9 Second World War, 3.10 POWs, 3.12 Medals, 3.13 War Graves

3.4 Militia Men

There were various systems for mustering local forces before the Militia Act of 1757 established formal militia regiments across England and Wales. These were essentially part-time voluntary forces, which were organized by county. The records of conscription (between 1758 and 1831) serve as a kind of census, as every year each parish was supposed to draw up lists of adult males, before holding a ballot to choose who would serve.

Militia Attestations Index 1860–1915, Findmypast
search.findmypast.co.uk/search-world-Records/british-army-service-records-1760-1915

This dataset was originally available from the Origins network, until it became part of the Findmypast family in 2014. Attestations were filled in at recruitment and contain lots of personal data. At the time of writing the collection included names of 110,000 recruits to militias across England, and south and central Scotland. Findmypast also has militia service records (1806–1915) from TNA WO 96.

Militia Guide, The National Archives
nationalarchives.gov.uk/records/research-guides/armed-forces-1522-1914.htm

Guide to records of officers/soldiers who served with the militia between 1522 and 1907. You can also search TNA's own records of disability pensions (WO 116), long service pensions (WO 117), enrolment and casualty books (WO 68), muster rolls and paylists (WO 13) and the Militia Long Service and Good Conduct Medal records (WO 102/22).

Hertfordshire Militia, Hertfordshire FHS
hertsfhs.org.uk/hfphs7.html

As militia lists are often the nearest thing to a pre-census census, you may find they have been indexed and/or transcribed by the local genealogical society. Herts FHS, for example, initially issued 112 booklets containing 280,000 militia records, which have now been combined into this single CD-Rom.

Rifles Berkshire and Wiltshire Museum

thewardrobe.org.uk/research/soldier-search/search

It's worth seeing what relevant regimental museums hold. The Rifles Museum's Soldier Search page, for example, incorporates the Militia Directory, which will sometimes give details of birthplace, plus place, date and age on enlistment. To find more army museums go to: armymuseums.org.uk.

Discovery, The National Archives

discovery.nationalarchives.gov.uk

Since incorporating A2A, Discovery is the place to trawl for militia material in local archives. Try searching with the word 'militia', then choose 'Other Archives' from the results. You can then further narrow by date range and repository.

Militia Lists, TheGenealogist

thegenealogist.co.uk/featuredarticles/2013/militia-records-121/

Guide to using militia records available through TheGenealogist. It launched its collection of English and Welsh militia muster lists in 2013, including over 58,000 records. The site also hosts various army lists.

Loyal Tay Fencibles, Fife FHS

fifefhs.org/resources/records

This page has free downloads from the society which include an article and transcription of Loyal Tay Fencibles.

The Gazette

www.thegazette.co.uk

The Gazette published details of appointments and commissions for militia officers.

Royal Lancashire Regiment, Register of Recruits 1779–82, Manchester Archives

manchester.gov.uk/downloads/download/4205/royal_lancashire_regiment

PDF of a booklet with a transcribed list of recruits.

Ross and Cromarty Militia

freepages.genealogy.rootsweb.ancestry.com/~coigach/

Militia lists from Lochbroom in Ross and Cromarty, dating from 1798, 1821 and 1825–7.

Hampshire Militia, Archives Guide

www3.hants.gov.uk/archives/hals-collections/militia-lists.htm

An example of the kind of holdings that may survive at your local record office.

Devon Militia Lists, Genuki

genuki.cs.ncl.ac.uk/DEV/DevonMisc/MilitiaLists/index.html

This is just one example of lots of militia-related material that you can find through Genuki.

Militia Records, GenGuide
genguide.co.uk/source/militia-records-military/87/

Military Records Guide, National Archives of Scotland
nas.gov.uk/guides/military.asp

See also: 3.1 Army, 3.5 Napoleonic Wars, 3.6 Victorian Wars

3.5 Napoleonic Wars

Unlike various coalition partners, Britain remained at war with France throughout the period of the Napoleonic Wars that fell between 1803 and 1814. Some army and navy records from the era have been digitized, plus there are very detailed websites that focus on individual battles, commanders, vessels and more.

Trafalgar Ancestors, The National Archives
apps.nationalarchives.gov.uk/trafalgarancestors/

Free National Archives database of more than 18,000 individuals who fought in the Battle of Trafalgar, drawn mainly from ships' musters. Results include service histories and biographical details, where known. Searching by the name Scott, for example, led to 34-year-old Carlisle-born Andrew Scott, a sailmaker's mate aboard HMS *Victory*, who later served on HMS *Ocean*.

Peninsular Roll Call, Napoleon Series
napoleon-series.org/research/biographies/GreatBritain/Challis/c_ChallisIntro.html

This address takes you direct to the Peninsular Roll Call – an index of officers who served with Wellington's army. It was originally compiled by Captain Lionel Challis, who began working on the project soon after the First World War. Vast parent website the Napoleon Series was launched in 1995 and boasts articles, images, maps, reviews and lots more.

Royal Navy Officers, The National Archives
nationalarchives.gov.uk/records/royal-naval-officers-service-records.htm

This site takes you to the Royal Navy officers' service records (1756–1931) search page. Wills of Royal Navy and Royal Marines personnel (1786–1882) can be searched via Discovery. There are also several relevant TNA research guides which include British army operations up to 1913 and the Napoleonic Wars.

Trafalgar Roll, Genuki
genuki.org.uk/big/eng/Trafalgar/

Compiled from awards made to the seamen who fought in the various Royal Navy ships under Nelson. It also includes British Ships at Trafalgar, which lists commanding officers, crew and the number of casualties.

Waterloo Medal, Naval and Military Archives
nmarchive.com/our-data

Hosts the Men of the Battle of Waterloo database, which lists the individuals granted the Waterloo Medal. This was the first true campaign medal as it was given to all, regardless of rank, and was won by some 39,000 veterans.

Waterloo Roll Call, archive.org
archive.org/details/waterloorollcall00daltuoft

There are lots of digitized history books available through Archive.org. This address takes you to a second edition copy of the *Waterloo Roll Call*, 1904, with 'biographical notes and anecdotes'.

Peninsula Medal Roll, FamilyRelatives
familyrelatives.com/search/search_peninsula_medalroll.php

The Peninsular Medal Roll (1793–1814) lists more than 26,000 men, and generally records rank, regiment, number/particulars of clasps, and remarks.

Waterloo 200
waterloo200.org/links/

Focus of the bicentenary celebrations of the Battle of Waterloo. The links section leads to all kinds of useful genealogical websites.

Waterloo 1815
napoleon-battles.com

You may want to turn the sound down on your machine before visiting this website, which focuses primarily on the Battle of Waterloo.

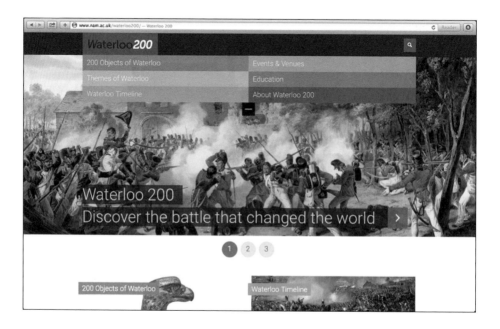

Napoleon's Army

napoleonistyka.atspace.com/BATTLE_OF_WATERLOO.htm

Military history site focusing on technical details of 'Napoleon, His Army and Enemies'. This page gives a detailed overview of the Battle of Waterloo.

Saint Helena Medal

stehelene.org

Free database of the medal that was awarded to soldiers still alive in 1857 who had fought with Napoleon between 1792 and 1815.

British Battles

britishbattles.com

Has a number of pages covering battles from the period, including details of casualties and uniforms.

Peninsular War

peninsularwar.org

An illustrated overview of the Peninsular War.

Waterloo Battlefield

waterloo1815.be/en/waterloo/

Official website of Waterloo battlefield.

Peninsular War 200

peninsularwar200.org

Friends of the British Cemetery, Elvas

british-cemetery-elvas.org

Officers Died Database

glosters.tripod.com/memindex3.htm

Nelson Society

nelson-society.com

Napoleonic Historical Society

napoleonichistoricalsociety.com

International Napoleonic Society

napoleonicsociety.com

See also: 3.1 Army, 3.2 Navy, 3.4 Militia Men, 3.6 Victorian Wars

3.6 Victorian Wars

These websites can help you research numerous nineteenth-century conflicts, which include ongoing wars with France and America, the Indian Mutiny, and the Anglo-Afghan, Zulu, Opium and Crimean wars.

Victorian Wars Forum

victorianwars.com

Bustling forum dedicated to British Military campaigns from 1837 to 1902. There are sections focusing on individual conflicts (the most active being the Boer War), while the most popular discussion area is Uniforms, Insignia, Equipment and Medals; there's also a dedicated topic called Researching Individual Soldiers and Sailors, where you can post any genealogical queries.

British Battles

britishbattles.com

The number of ads here is a little annoying, but if you ignore them there's lots of fascinating content. You can explore the battles by date range, and most have accompanying images that include paintings, battle plans and associated campaign medals.

Second Anglo-Afghan War

garenewing.co.uk/angloafghanwar/

History of the Second Anglo-Afghan War (1878–80) by illustrator and designer Garen Ewing. This includes the Second Afghan War database project – a collection of names, family histories and stories concerning those who participated in the campaign.

Indian Mutiny Medal Roll, FIBIS

search.fibis.org/frontis/bin/

This is the dedicated Families in British India Society database site. Scroll down the Browse Records bar on the left, then choose Military Records > Medal Rolls to find the Indian Mutiny Medal Roll.

Zulu War, National Army Museum

nam.ac.uk/exhibitions/online-exhibitions/zulu-war-1879

NAM online exhibition dedicated to the 1879 Zulu War. Through the museum's Online Collection (nam.ac.uk/online-collection/) you can also browse all kinds of artefacts and images relating to various Victorian conflicts.

British Battles: From Crimea to Korea, The National Archives

nationalarchives.gov.uk/battles/

This is the TNA's dedicated battle exhibition page. Key research guides to the era include British army muster rolls and pay lists c.1730–1898 (nationalarchives. gov.uk/records/research-guides/army-muster-1730-1898.htm).

Victorian Conflict, Findmypast

findmypast.co.uk

This site offers the likes of TNA's Chelsea Pensioners' Records, Militia Attestation Papers (1806–1915) and Soldiers' Service Documents (1760–1913).

Forces War Records

forces-war-records.co.uk

At time of writing, this specialist commercial site boasted 391,553 Boer War records, 38,000 records relating to the Crimean War, and 135,000 early nineteenth-century records.

British Newspaper Archives

blog.britishnewspaperarchive.co.uk/2013/10/24/charge-light-brigade/

Explore contemporary coverage of all conflicts from the period. This address leads to the site's official blog, quoting accounts from the Charge of the Light Brigade.

Britain's Small Forgotten Wars

britainssmallwars.co.uk

Fascinating look at some of the more obscure conflicts from the past 200 years, with particular reference to any surviving memorials.

Soldiers of the Queen

soldiersofthequeen.com

Virtual museum of Victorian-era British military photographs.

Military Campaign Medal and Award Rolls (1793–1949), Ancestry

search.ancestry.co.uk/search/db.aspx?dbid=1686

Officers Died Database
glosters.tripod.com/memindex3.htm

Crimean War Research Society
cwrs.russianwar.co.uk

Anglo Zulu War Historical Society
anglozuluwar.com

British Army in Bermuda
bermuda-online.org/britarmy.htm

Rorke's Drift VC
rorkesdriftvc.com

Victorian Military History Society
victorianmilitarysociety.org.uk

Royal Artillery Museum
firepower.org.uk

Royal Engineers Museum
remuseum.org.uk

British Empire
britishempire.co.uk

British Medal Forum
britishmedalforum.com

See also: 3.1 Army, 3.2 Navy, 3.4 Militia Men, 3.5 Napoleonic Wars, 3.7 Boer Wars

3.7 Boer Wars

Two separate Boer Wars were fought between the British Empire and two independent Boer states. The one commonly referred to as the 'Boer War' is in fact the second, which took place between 1899 and 1902. It was the biggest deployment of British troops since the Crimea, involving half a million soldiers, including volunteers from Canada, Australia and New Zealand.

Anglo-Boer War
angloboerwar.com

This site celebrated a decade online in 2014, and has articles on honours and awards, thousands of images, useful information on the likes of the Queen's South Africa Medal (and index), plus biographical information on many people involved in the conflict, and details of units that participated. It currently boasts 361,000 soldiers' records, a forum with 23,000 posts, plus 85 free-to-view books.

Register of the Anglo-Boer War 1899–1902
casus-belli.co.uk

The 'premier research resource' for everyone interested in the participants of the conflict. The data can be purchased direct from this website, or explored through Findmypast. It also hosts the Anglo-Boer War Memorials Project (casus-belli.co.uk/abwmp/), which records memorials across the world and currently has over 200,000 names.

Boer War Roll of Honour
roll-of-honour.com/Boer/

This page details the scope of the Boer Roll of Honour database, and suggests alternate online sources if the name you're looking for doesn't appear. The right-hand column leads to details of UK Boer War memorials.

Campaign Medals 1793–1949, Ancestry
ancestry.co.uk/cs/uk/military

Ancestry's campaign medals database is useful for researching the subject. They also have UK Casualties of the Boer War (originally on Military-Genealogy.com), which records 55,000 British soldiers killed, captured or wounded.

Anglo-Boer War Records, Findmypast
search.findmypast.co.uk/search-world-records/anglo-boer-war-records-1899-1902

This database contains 271,771 names drawn from various sources, and should reveal your ancestor's unit and any medals/awards won. The register also contains 59,000 casualty records.

Boer War Guide, The National Archives
nationalarchives.gov.uk/records/looking-for-subject/boerwar.htm

Brief guide to governmental and military records of the Second Boer War – which are summarized as 'wide-ranging and fragmented'.

Manchester Regiment Archives on the Boer War
www.tameside.gov.uk/leisure/new/lh39.htm

Tameside Local Studies and Archives Centre's description of the Manchester Regiment Archives relating to the Boer War.

Victorian Wars
victorianwars.com

The Boer War represents the busiest section of this specialist forum.

The Gazette
www.thegazette.co.uk

Find references to gallantry awards.

Concentration Camps of the Boer War
web.stanford.edu/dept/SUL/library/prod//depts/ssrg/africa/boers.html

Index of Soldiers, Sailors and Nurses in the Second Anglo-Boer War
members.pcug.org.au/~croe/sotq/welcome.html

National Army Museum
national-army-museum.ac.uk

Anglo-Boer War Museum
www.anglo-boer.co.za

British Medal Forum
britishmedalforum.com

See also: 3.1 Army, 3.2 Navy, 3.6 Victorian Wars, 3.12 Medals

3.8 First World War

First World War history was already well catered for before the centenary, which has seen the launch of vast UK- and Europe-wide crowdsourcing projects, plus lots of local digital commemorations. There's never been a better time to delve into and share your family's experiences of the conflict.

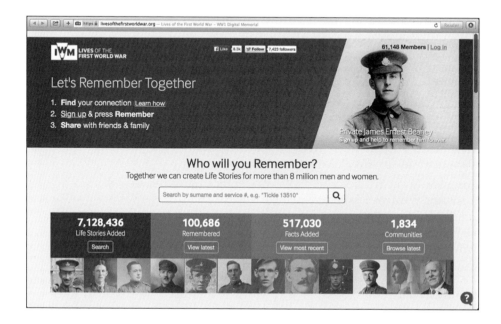

Lives of the First World War

livesofthefirstworldwar.org

This expanding centenary crowdsourcing project ultimately aims to record as many as possible of the individuals who contributed to the war effort – both overseas and on the home front. Joining, browsing and uploading life stories can all be done for free, but subscribers can access various 'premium record sets' (available on Findmypast) and create online communities.

Commonwealth War Graves Commission

cwgc.org

Searchable database of service personnel who died during both world wars. The commission also has a dedicated microsite, Discover 14–18 (www.cwgc.org/discover1418), with history articles and advice for researchers. In 2014 it launched casualty archive documents – access to a further 300,000 digitized documents relating to grave registration, exhumation, verification, headstones and more.

First World War 100, The National Archives

nationalarchives.gov.uk/first-world-war/

TNA military holdings are detailed elsewhere, but there are also research guides to non-military sources such as those related to conscientious objectors. Meanwhile the above address takes you to TNA's dedicated First World War centenary site; there's also the older 'Sources for History' sub-site (nationalarchives.gov.uk/pathways/firstworldwar/index.htm).

The Long, Long Trail

1914-1918.net

This site is dedicated to researching the British army during the First World War, and it is aimed squarely at family historians. It boasts details of regiments, formations, battles, army life and regulations, plus there's the Researching a Soldier guide, and hidden gems such as the 'Behind the Wire' database of POWs (1914-1918.net/POW/other_pow.php).

First World War Portal, Ancestry

ancestry.co.uk/world-war-1

From here you will find several key collections such as Service Records (1914–20), First World War Army Pension Records, Medal Records, Naval Service Records (1802–1919) and more. Ancestry has also launched WebSearch projects such as the Women's Royal Naval Service Index and the Women's Army Auxiliary Corps Index.

Western Front Association

westernfrontassociation.com

This is a fantastic website from a thriving historical group, with interesting sections and articles on the history of the war on land, at sea and in the air. Rotating homepage signposts lead to all kinds of content – from female army pay-office volunteers to the Halifax explosion of December 1917.

Welsh Experience of the First World War

cymru1914.org

Mass digitization project which draws on material held in libraries and archives across Wales, to create this free digital resource. You can search the entire collection or browse by type of record: newspapers, archives and manuscripts, photographs, journals or sound.

First World War Portal, Findmypast

findmypast.co.uk/ww1

This is FMP's dedicated launch page for all things First World War, including records of soldiers who died in the Great War, newspapers, plus non-military and military sources such as service records of British army officers, Royal Navy officers/seamen and RAF airmen.

Red Cross Voluntary Aid Detachment

redcross.org.uk/ww1

The British Red Cross's Voluntary Aid Detachment (VAD) records. The site launched in 2014 with 30,000 records – with a further 236,000 due over the year. You can the check progress of the project and view material on famous volunteers such as Agatha Christie and Algernon Blackwood, plus sections describing the VAD's work, auxiliary hospitals and food parcels.

First World War Centenary

1914.org

Led by IWM, this is the place to keep track of centenary events and online projects between 2014 and 2018. Really helpful for finding local projects that might be relevant to your family's history.

Inventory of War Memorials

iwm.org.uk/memorials/search

Database of war memorials located throughout the United Kingdom, Channel Islands and Isle of Man. Has recorded more than 65,000 (of an approximated 100,000) to date.

Europeana 1914–1918

europeana1914-1918.eu/

Explore letters, diaries, photographs, films, documents and more through this Europe-wide project, which mixes archive/library resources with crowdsourced memories and memorabilia.

First World War Galleries, Imperial War Museum

iwm.org.uk/exhibitions/iwm-london/first-world-war-galleries

Find out more about IWM London's new First World War galleries. You can also try iwm.org.uk/history-terms/first-world-war, which shows various sections related to the subject.

First World War Newspapers, British Newspaper Archive

blog.britishnewspaperarchive.co.uk/tag/world-war-1/

This page lists First World War-related entries in the official britishnewspaper archive.co.uk blog, including an article looking at contemporary reports of the Christmas truce.

Operation War Diary

operationwardiary.org

Crowdsourcing project from Zooniverse, IWM and TNA, aiming to uncover stories from unit war diaries from the Western Front.

First World War in Focus, National Army Museum

nam.ac.uk/microsites/ww1/

The museum's microsite includes the expanding Soldiers' Stories section, which follows the experiences of individual soldiers.

Canadian Soldiers, First World War

bac-lac.gc.ca/eng/discover/military-heritage/first-world-war/first-world-war-1914-1918-cef/Pages/canadian-expeditionary-force.aspx

Ongoing digitization of the Canadian Expeditionary Force (CEF) service files. You can also search the current database.

First World War Centenary, National Maritime Museum

rmg.co.uk/whats-on/ww1-centenary

The museum's Forgotten Fighters gallery highlights some of the lesser-known stories of the war at sea.

Naval-History.net

naval-history.net

Vast website with all kinds of material on Royal Navy dispatches, honours and awards, operations, battles and more.

Every Man Remembered

everymanremembered.org

Royal British Legion and CWGC joint project to commemorate those who fell in the First World War.

Trench Maps, National Library of Scotland

maps.nls.uk/ww1/trenches

Access high-resolution zoomable images of First World War trench maps.

Discover World War One, Archives New Zealand

archives.govt.nz/world-war-one

Home to more than 141,000 New Zealand Defence Force records.

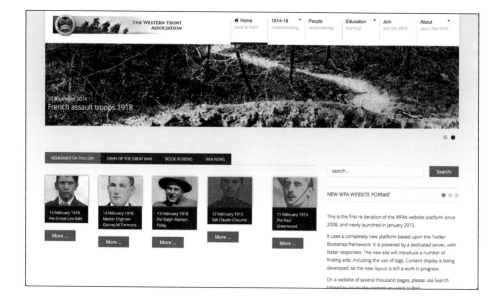

British Army War Diaries 1914–1922
nationalarchives.gov.uk / records / war-diaries-ww1.htm

Selected collection of digitized war diaries of units in the British army.

BBC History
bbc.co.uk / history / british / britain_wwone /

Explores seismic changes to British society during the conflict.

Centenary, GOV.UK
www.gov.uk / government / topical-events / first-world-war-centenary

Official government website charting centenary commemorations.

Great War Forum
1914-1918.invisionzone.com /

Forum dedicated to First World War military research.

Glasgow Roll of Honour, Mitchell Library
glasgowfamilyhistory.org.uk

Details of the *Evening Times* Roll of Honour.

Ruhleben Civilian Internment Camp
ruhleben.tripod.com

Tells the story of British internees at Ruhleben in Germany.

Great War
greatwar.co.uk
Guide to battlefields and history.

FirstWorldWar.com
firstworldwar.com
A 'multimedia history' of the First World War.

First World War Wounded Collection, TheGenealogist
thegenealogist.co.uk/ww1-wounded

First World War Centenary, HistoryPin
historypin.org/firstworldwar

World War 1 Naval Combat
worldwar1.co.uk

Macclesfield Reflects
macclesfieldreflects.org.uk

BBC Centenary Coverage
bbc.co.uk/ww1

See also 3.1 Army, 3.2 Navy, 3.3 RAF, 3.10 POWs, 3.11 Home Front, 3.12 Medals, 3.13 War Graves

3.9 Second World War

The digital projects commemorating First World War centenaries have rather swamped Second World War content. But while the military records aren't as accessible as their First World War counterparts, there's still plenty of material available for genealogists looking into an individual's wartime service.

Second World War Records Guide, The National Archives
nationalarchives.gov.uk/records/looking-for-subject/secondworldwar.htm

Guide to records available here, plus there's the rather dated (but still interesting) education section at nationalarchives.gov.uk/education/worldwar2/default.htm. There's also the evacuees research guide at nationalarchives.gov.uk/records/research-guides/home-front-1939-1945.htm.

Second World War, Imperial War Museum
iwm.org.uk/history/second-world-war

This lists online exhibitions touching on the home front and overseas theatres. It's well illustrated with sections on the Blitz, Operation Market Garden, evacuated children, life in Nazi Germany and propaganda posters. You can also search the catalogue (iwm.org.uk/collections/search) of 600,000 items – 90,000 of which have digitized images, sound or video attached.

1939 Register
1939register.co.uk

The register was compiled by the British government shortly after the outbreak of war, and was used to issue identity cards, organize rationing and later to set up the National Health Service. This is the only large-scale population survey to cover the years between 1921 and 1951, and it is due to launch in late 2015.

TA Divisions, Wikipedia
en.wikipedia.org/wiki/Territorial_Army_(United_Kingdom)

Useful Wikipedia entry which tells the story of what is now called the Army Reserve, before listing TA divisions during the Second World War.

Army Roll of Honour, Naval and Military Archives
nmarchive.com/our-data

Naval and Military Press spin-off site that has the 1939–45 Army Roll of Honour (171,214 records).

Women of the Air Force, RAF Museum
rafmuseum.org.uk/research/online-exhibitions/women-of-the-air-force.aspx

Exhibition which tells the story of the Women's Auxiliary Air Force and the Women's Royal Air Force.

British Pathé
britishpathe.com

Explore Second World War newsreels, video and archive film footage and stills.

Bomb Sight
bombsight.org

Explore London during wartime with this 'bomb census' of the Blitz.

Second World War, BBC History
bbc.co.uk/history/worldwars/wwtwo/

Concise narrative of the war.

Manchester Regiment
tameside.gov.uk/museumsgalleries/mom/history/territorial1939

This page focuses on TA battalions between 1920 and 1945.

WW2F
ww2f.com

Specialist forum focusing on Second World War history.

Second World War Collection, Forces War Records
forces-war-records.co.uk/ww2-records

Battle of Britain Memorial
battleofbritainmemorial.org/events/

Operation Market Garden, National Army Museum
nam.ac.uk/exhibitions/online-exhibitions/operation-market-garden

Kent Battle of Britain Museum
kbobm.org

Commonwealth War Graves Commission
www.cwgc.org/about-us/history-of-cwgc/second-world-war.aspx

Bletchley Park
bletchleypark.org.uk

War Memorials Search, IWM
iwm.org.uk/memorials/search

War Graves Photographic Project
twgpp.org

Britain at War
www.britain-at-war.org.uk

World War 2 Planes
world-war-2-planes.com

See also 3.1 Army, 3.2 Navy, 3.3 RAF, 3.10 POWs, 3.11 Home Front, 3.12 Medals, 3.13 War Graves

3.10 POWs

It is estimated that during the First World War, 10 million people (including servicemen and civilians) were captured and detained – including some 7,000+ officers and 174,000+ other ranks of the British army. And by the end of the Second World War, in the Far East alone, more than 190,000 Allied servicemen were prisoners of the Japanese.

POW Guide, The National Archives
nationalarchives.gov.uk/records/looking-for-person/britishpowfirstworldwar.htm
The main research guides are British POWs c.1790–1919, British Prisoners of the Second World War and Korean War, and Prisoners in British hands. These detail sources available off and online. Via TNA you can also search/download (for a fee) POW interviews/reports (1914–20), or via Discovery search Foreign Office reports (1915–19) and a 1943 list of army POWs in Germany and occupied territories.

Prisoners of the First World War
grandeguerre.icrc.org

Search ICRG (International Committee of the Red Cross) lists of First World War POWs from both sides of the conflict. You can first narrow your search by nationality, or just carry out a name search. Results can include items such as enquiry cards from next of kin and images, repatriation lists and accounts of the camps.

Where To Find POW Records, Imperial War Museum
iwm.org.uk/collections-research/tracing-your-family-history/prisoners-of-war/where-to-find-prisoner-of-war-records

Museum guide to POW records, most of which are held at TNA. IWM also preserves personal papers/diaries, camp journals, photographs, artworks and recorded interviews, which you find via the online catalogue at: iwm.org.uk/collections-research.

Naval and Military Archives
nmarchive.com/our-data

This page details the holdings from the Naval and Military Press spin-off site, which comprise three Second World War POW datasets containing more than 160,000 records, plus British Officers Taken POW August 1914 to November 1918, containing a further 8,300.

Stalag VIIIB
lamsdorf.com

Dedicated to one of the biggest camps of the Second World War – Stalag VIIIB (later renumbered 344) at Lamsdorf in Poland, which held up to 48,000 prisoners.

Forces War Records
forces-war-records.co.uk

Datasets include Prisoners of War of the British Empire held in Germany 1939–45, drawn from TNA sources, and Imperial Prisoners of War held in Italy 1943.

Lamsdorf Remembered
lamsdorfremembered.co.uk

Site built around *Sojourn in Silesia* by former Irish Guard Arthur Charles Evans, which recounts his POW experiences in Stalag VIIIB.

The Gazette
www.thegazette.co.uk

You can check *London Gazette* references to British POWs captured during the Crimean and Boer wars. These are incomplete and generally name officers only.

Children and Families of Far East POW
cofepowdb.org.uk

A database of Far East POWs, containing basic information and a copy of each prisoner's liberation questionnaire – if completed. Currently has around 55,500 names.

Stalag Luft I Online
merkki.com

A collection of stories, photos and information about Stalag Luft I in Barth, Germany, which held approximately 8,939 Allied Airmen – 7,588 Americans and 1,351 RAF.

POW Taiwan
powtaiwan.org

The story of camps on the island of Taiwan (Formosa) during WWII. There's also a roll of honour for men who died while resident.

RAF Escaping Society Museum
www.rafinfo.org.uk/rafescape/rafesmus.html

Includes replicas of the 'Wooden Horse' used to escape from Stalag Luft III and the 'Colditz Glider'.

Buckden Pike Memorial Cross
buckdenpike.co.uk

Contains an account of the infamous Lamsdorf Death March, March 1945.

Stalag 18A
stalag18a.org.uk

Information about Stalag 18A, Wolfsberg, Austria.

The Great Escape, Stalag Luft 3
www.ateal.co.uk/greatescape/

Wartime experiences of Wing Commander H.K. Rees.

TheGenealogist
thegenealogist.co.uk

Launched a major new WW1 POW database in 2014.

Finding Records of British POWs, The Long, Long Trail
1914-1918.net/soldiers/powrecords.html

The National Ex-Prisoner of War Association
prisonerofwar.org.uk

British POWs 1939–45, Ancestry
ancestry.co.uk/search/db.aspx?dbid=1601

Laghouat POW Camp, Algeria
www.wartimememoriesproject.com/ww2/pow/laghouat.php#jtbrown

Stalag, Prisoners of Germany
stalag.weebly.com

Prisoners of Italy
powsitaly.weebly.com

Prisoners in the Far East
powsfareast.weebly.com

Stalag VIIIb
stalag-viiib.com

See also: 3.8 First World War, 3.9 Second World War

3.11 Home Front

There's never been a better time to research life on the home front. You'll soon discover that life for the average home guard or land girl recruit was more gruelling then the propaganda would have us believe.

Imperial War Museum, 1914.org
1914.org

The Imperial War Museum's centenary hub has news of projects commemorating sacrifice on the home front. Meanwhile the museum's own Home Front page (iwm.org.uk/history/first-world-war-home-front) has galleries exploring women's war work, rationing and food shortages, state controls, air raids and the impact of the Defence of the Realm Act. There's a not so up-to-date Second World War equivalent, plus this page focusing on the Home Guard: iwm.org.uk/history/the-home-guard.

1939 Register
1939register.co.uk

Due to go live at the end of 2015 (or early 2016) this is the nearest we'll come to a census of individuals in Britain in 1939, making it a vital source for researching home front ancestors. The register was compiled by the British government to issue identity cards and organize rationing, and was later used to set up the National Health Service. It is being digitized by Findmypast, in association with TNA, and records more than 40 million Britons who were alive on 29 September 1939.

Conscientious Objectors, The National Archives
nationalarchives.gov.uk/records/looking-for-person/conscientiousobjectors.htm

Potential home front sources preserved at TNA include material relating to conscientious objectors, Voluntary Aid Detachments (VADs), nursing service records, and campaign medal records (1914–20). There's also the evacuees research guide at nationalarchives.gov.uk/records/looking-for-person/evacuees.htm.

Coventry at War
www.familyresearcher.co.uk/Coventry-At-War/Coventry-At-War.html

Includes sections on the Humber Home Guard and the 16th Warwickshire (Coventry) Battalion Home Guard, with photos and transcribed documents that show the kind of evidence which may survive in smaller archives. There's also an index to victims of the devastating Coventry Blitz.

People's War

bbc.co.uk/ww2peopleswar/

Archived section of a BBC mass-observation project with 47,000 stories relating to the Second World War, which were compiled between 2003 and 2006. These include sections on the Land Army, Family Life, Home Guard, Fire Duty and Conscientious Objectors.

Commonwealth War Graves Commission

www.cwgc.org/find-war-dead.aspx

The CWGC casualty database also records details of the 67,000 Commonwealth civilians who died 'as a result of enemy action' in the Second World War. From the above page you can choose to concentrate your search solely on civilian casualties.

Films from the Home Front

www.movinghistory.ac.uk/homefront/index.html

Brings together film clips illustrating life for ordinary people during the Second World War through amateur documentaries, newsreels, government films and home movies.

Home Guard Records, Forces War Records

forces-war-records.co.uk/collections/85/home-guard-officer-lists-1939-45/

Has 'exclusively transcribed' TNA's Home Guard Officer Lists (1939–45) and the Home Guard Auxiliary Units (1939–45).

Rotherwas Munitions Hereford

rotherwasmunitionshereford.co.uk

A group dedicated to preserving the memory of employees at the Royal Ordinance Factory in Rotherwas, Hereford, where some 12,000 men and women worked during both world wars.

Home Front, Wikipedia

en.wikipedia.org/wiki/Home_front_during_World_War_I

Also links to more detailed sections on specific occurrences such as raids on Scarborough, Hartlepool and Whitby.

Lives of the First World War

livesofthefirstworldwar.org

This crowdsourcing project is designed to remember those who served on the home front as well as overseas.

Great War Archive

europeana1914-1918.eu

Collections of pictures, letters, postcards, artefacts and stories relating to the First World War, which illustrates life at home and at the front.

Wartime Memories Project

www.wartimememoriesproject.com/ww2/homefront/index.php

Volunteer-run project which is forming a growing digital archive of memories/stories relating to both world wars.

HistoryPin

historypin.com/collections/

It's worth searching HistoryPin by subject or collection to see what home front material has been posted.

Folkestone Raid, 1917

freepages.genealogy.rootsweb.ancestry.com/~folkestonefamilies/Tontinestreet.htm

Rootsweb-hosted description of the devastating 1917 air raid on Folkestone.

Wolverhampton History

wolverhamptonhistory.org.uk/people/at_war/ww1/home_front

Covers the home front during both world wars.

Gorleston History

gorlestonhistory.org.uk/worldwars/zeppelinairraid1915.php

Read about Zeppelin attacks in Norfolk in 1915.

Home Sweet Home Front

homesweethomefront.co.uk

Women's Land Army

womenslandarmy.co.uk

Women's Land Army Tribute

www.womenslandarmytribute.co.uk

Land Army

landarmy.org.uk

Land Girls and Lumber Jills, Scotland's National War Museum

www.nms.ac.uk/our_museums/war_museum/land_girls_and_lumber_jills.aspx

First World War, Home Front

firstworldwar.com/photos/homefront.htm

TyneLives

tynelives.org.uk/war/home.htm

Bath Blitz

bathblitz.org

See also: 3.8 First World War, 3.9 Second World War

3.12 Medals

Sources relating to medals have been digitized by several of the big commercial players. Plus the online community of enthusiasts and collectors means there's a huge amount of exhaustive and detailed information to help you identify campaign medals, medals for valour and all kinds of military insignia.

Medals, The National Archives

nationalarchives.gov.uk/records/medals.htm

TNA's online collections of medal records include British Army Medal Index Cards (1914–20), merchant seamen's campaign medal records (1914–18 and 1939–45) and the Victoria Cross Registers. There are also various medal research guides, for example: nationalarchives.gov.uk/records/research-guides/medals-british-armed-services-gallantry.htm, which includes a useful table of awards, with links to the TNA record series and external online sources such as the *London Gazette*.

The Military Medal, TheGenealogist

thegenealogist.co.uk/military-medal

Over 117,000 military medals were awarded for 'acts of gallantry and devotion to duty under fire' during the First World War. Here you can view images of the actual medal cards, plus a link to the official government notification in *The Gazette*. The site also has the 25,000 records of Non-Commissioned Officers and Other Ranks who were awarded the Distinguished Conduct Medal during the Boer War and the First World War.

Medals, Ancestry

ancestry.co.uk/cs/uk/military

Find out more about Ancestry's medal sources, created in partnership with TNA, which include British army First World War medal rolls index cards (1914–20). There's also the campaign medals (1793–1949) database.

Medals of the World

medals.org.uk

Longstanding (but no longer updated) collection of images of medals from around the world. Most of the UK-related military medals here include photographs of the obverse and reverse of the award, plus a graphic showing the official ribbon.

Medals, Findmypast

search.findmypast.co.uk/search-world-records/world-war-one-british-army-medal-index-cards

This section has British army medal index cards, the Royal Naval Volunteer Reserve medal roll, the Royal Artillery military medal awards, Royal Navy officers' medal roll (1914–20), First World War Distinguished Conduct Medal citations and more.

Anglo-Boer War
angloboerwar.com

Has biographies of all recipients of the DSO and VC, various naval awards, and pages dedicated to specific medals such as the Afghan War Medal.

Victoria Cross, Wikipedia
en.wikipedia.org/wiki/Victoria_Cross

Learn more about the history of specific medals and decorations: this example relates to the most famous of all.

The British Campaign Medals of WW1, The Long, Long Trail
1914-1918.net/soldiers/themedals.html

Long, Long Trail page which gives details of the various medals of the First World War.

British Medals Forum
britishmedalforum.com

Covers British, Canadian, Australian, New Zealand, Indian, South African and all Commonwealth medals.

Victorian Wars Forum
victorianwars.com

By far the most popular section relates to Uniforms, Insignia, Equipment and Medals.

Victoria Cross
www.victoriacross.org.uk

Includes an index to VC holders and details of the location of graves of VC holders.

Medal Records guide, IWM
iwm.org.uk/collections-and-research/tracing-your-family-history/tracing-your-royal-flying-corps-and-royal-air/medal-records

The Imperial War Museum's clear and concise introduction to medal records.

British Armed Forces
britisharmedforces.org

Has galleries and images of regimental badges.

Orders and Medals Research Society
omrs.org.uk

Australian Armed Services
asacaustralia.com

Gentleman's Military Interest Club
gmic.co.uk

Ribbons of Orders and Decorations of the World
medals.pl

Regimental Army Museums
armymuseums.org.uk

Medal Tracker
medaltracker.com

Orders, Decorations and Medals
www.jeanpaulleblanc.com/Britain.htm

Victoria Cross Society
victoriacrosssociety.com

US Army Centre of Military History, Medal of Honor Recipients
history.army.mil/moh/index.html

See also 3.1 Army, 3.2 Navy, 3.3 RAF, 3.5 Napoleonic Wars, 3.6 Victorian Wars, 3.7 Boer Wars, 3.8 First World War, 3.9 Second World War

3.13 War Graves

The Commonwealth War Graves Commission Debt of Honour Register is the single most important website documenting the war dead. But there are lots of global and regional projects dedicated to photographing and transcribing memorials across counties, towns and villages – and others that tell the stories behind the names etched in stone.

Commonwealth War Graves Commission

www.cwgc.org

The site has become more smart and streamlined in recent years, and various useful search options have been added, such as the ability to search by unit. At its heart is the database of 1.7 million men and women of the Commonwealth forces who died, and the 23,000 cemeteries, memorials and other locations worldwide where they are commemorated. You can filter results by a huge number of fields including regiment, service number and rank. Plus in 2014 further archive documents were added, granting access to around 300,000 digitized documents relating to grave registration, exhumation, verification, headstones and more.

Diamond War Memorial, Derry

diamondwarmemorial.com

Fascinating project in which a local historian uncovered approximately 400 names that had been overlooked from the memorial in Derry. The database includes the full list – both those commemorated and those omitted – and a huge amount of further information is recorded about each person, often including family and connections.

War Memorials Search, IWM

iwm.org.uk/memorials/search

Project to compile a record of all war memorials across the UK – from community crosses to school plaques – which aims to cover all conflicts. Successful searches lead to a satellite image, OS grid reference, memorial type, plus subject/period (for example: 'Non-combat deaths, WW2'), a description and transcription.

War Graves Photographic Project

twgpp.org

The original aim of this project was to build a photographic database of every single war grave, memorial and MoD grave from the First World War to the present day. However, the site states that due to its popularity: 'we have now extended our remit to cover all nationalities and military conflicts'.

TheGenealogist

thegenealogist.co.uk

TheGenealogist has its own Headstone Project, to which more material from war memorials and cemeteries is being added. (There's also a mobile Headstone App, allowing users to more easily record information from local cemeteries.)

In From the Cold

infromthecold.org

This project tracks down details of individuals missing from the CWGC Debt of Honour Register. The total number of cases submitted by IFCP and accepted for commemoration by CWGC had exceeded 2,000 at the time of writing.

Irish War Memorials Project
irishwarmemorials.ie

Growing inventory of war memorials in the Republic of Ireland and Northern Ireland. It includes photographs of each memorial and PDF transcriptions of the text, often with further information about the names that appear.

Battle of Britain Memorial
battleofbritainmemorial.org

Saw lots of activity during the build-up to the seventy-fifth anniversary in 2015. It's also home to the Memorial Wall, which is engraved with the names of all those who were awarded the Battle of Britain Clasp.

Roll of Honour
roll-of-honour.com

Lots of useful data, links and photographs/transcriptions of memorials across the UK, organized by county.

WW1 Cemeteries
ww1cemeteries.com

Has photographs of 940 cemeteries in France and Belgium, plus an extensive 1939–45 Index with over 500 cemeteries.

Friends of Medway Archives
foma-lsc.org

Includes a recently compiled database of First World War soldiers commemorated in Medway memorials.

American Battle Monuments Commission
abmc.gov

Honouring more than '218,000 individuals buried or memorialized at our sites throughout the world.'

Buckinghamshire Remembers
buckinghamshireremembers.org.uk

Growing database of Great War casualties listed on Buckinghamshire's war memorials.

Derry~Londonderry War Memorial, PRONI
www.proni.gov.uk/index/search_the_archives/corporationarchive-3/warmemorial.htm

Digitized memorial records from the Derry~Londonderry War Memorial.

Veterans Affairs Canada
veterans.gc.ca

Includes the Canadian Virtual War Memorial to more than 118,000 Canadians and Newfoundlanders.

North East War Memorials Project
newmp.org.uk

Memorials located in Northumberland, Newcastle upon Tyne and County Durham.

British War Graves
britishwargraves.co.uk

Expanding volunteer-led photographic database of of war graves.

In Memory
inmemories.com

Dedicated to cemeteries throughout France and Belgium.

War Graves and Memorials in New Zealand
wargraves.co.nz

Dover War Memorial Project
doverwarmemorialproject.org.uk

Kent Fallen
kentfallen.com

Anglo-Boer War Memorials Project
casus-belli.co.uk/abwmp/index.html

Australian War Memorial
awm.gov.au

Every Man Remembered
everymanremembered.org

South Africa War Graves Project
southafricawargraves.org

Maple Leaf Legacy Project
mapleleaflegacy.ca

See also: 2.1 Burial Records and Monumental Inscriptions, 3.1 Army, 3.2 Navy, 3.3 RAF, 3.8 First World War, 3.9 Second World War, 3.12 Medals

Section 4

OCCUPATIONS

4.1 Miners

To find a working miner you need to focus on region, then company or pit – information you may already have to hand if you have found your ancestor in the census. The popular fascination with our industrial heritage means there are lots of websites aimed at both genealogists and mining-history enthusiasts.

Scottish Mining
scottishmining.co.uk

This site boasts a database of more than 22,000 names of those involved in coal, iron and shale mining across the country, drawn from gazetteers, newspapers and official accident reports. You can explore by parish via the left-hand menu, which leads to illustrated histories and details of accidents, memorials and more.

Durham Mining Museum
dmm.org.uk

Alongside general information aimed at visitors, this website hosts a vast amount of material not available elsewhere. There are mining histories; colliery maps; a who's who; lists of engineers; and all kinds of transcribed documents, including official reports into disasters and incidents in northern counties, and a handy master index to personal names mentioned on the site.

Mine Exploration Forum
aditnow.co.uk

Primarily aimed at industrial historians and enthusiasts, this encyclopaedic site is useful for finding out more about a particular mine. There's a mines database, which can be explored by name, region, mineral or via Google Maps, and the site boasts thousands of photographs, articles and documents.

Coal Mining History Resource Centre
cmhrc.co.uk

The CMHRC is a detailed and comprehensive source that boasts the National Database of Mining Deaths, compiled by Ian Winstanley, which dates back to the 1600s and includes more than 164,000 accidents and deaths. There are also PDF reports, location maps and more.

National Coal Mining Museum

ncm.org.uk

Includes details of the museum's reference library, plus under Collections you will find an online catalogue. Via sister site Online Resources, you can explore material such as digitized copies of the National Coal Board's official magazine *Coal*.

Scottish Mining Museum

scottishminingmuseum.com

The museum's reference library houses books, journals, trade catalogues and periodicals. There aren't any personnel records held here, but there is material relating to the Lothian Coal Company and the National Union of Mineworkers.

Tyne and Wear Archives Centre

twmuseums.org.uk/tyne-and-wear-archives/catalogue-amp-user-guides/user-guides.html

Research guides to material at the Tyne and Wear Archives Centre, including its coal-related material – such as colliery accounts, reports and photographs.

Mining guide, The National Archives

nationalarchives.gov.uk/records/research-guides/mines-and-mining.htm

The National Archives has no personnel records, but the guide details material relating to administration, nationalization, labour relations and more.

Peak District Mines Historical Society

pdmhs.com

Includes a general index to mines, references to local miners in the census, information on colliery accidents, plus photographs and newspaper clippings.

Australian Mining History Association

mininghistory.asn.au

History of mining from all over Australia, with a useful a bibliography, and a state-by-state description of mining history in Australia and New Zealand.

Cornish Mine Images

cornishmineimages.co.uk

Produced by amateur underground explorer and photographer Simon Jones, this site is the result of his passion for Cornwall, mining history and 35mm photography.

Cornwall Record Office

cornwall.gov.uk/community-and-living/records-archives-and-cornish-studies/cornwall-record-office/cornwall-record-office-collections/business-and-industries/mining/?page=14590

Summarizes the history of mining in Cornwall and explores the kinds of records that have survived.

Welsh Coal Mines

welshcoalmines.co.uk

Database of mines with histories and images collected by a former miner.

Coalfield Web Materials

agor.org.uk/cwm/

Explores the social, political and cultural life of the south Wales coalfield.

Digging up the Past

diggingupthepast.org.uk

Photographic history of coal mining in south Wales.

National Association of Mining History Organisations

namho.org

Includes a list of member groups from all over the UK.

Mindat

mindat.org

Encyclopaedic mineralogy reference database.

National Archives of Scotland, Mining guide

nas.gov.uk/guides/coalmining.asp

North of England Institute of Mining and Mechanical Engineers Library

mininginstitute.org.uk

Women and the Pits

freepages.genealogy.rootsweb.ancestry.com/~stenhouse/coal/pbl/coalmain.htm

Northern Mines Research Society

nmrs.org.uk

Welsh Mines Society
welshmines.org

Haig Colliery Mining Museum
visitcumbria.com/wc/haig-colliery-mining-museum/

Silverwood Colliery
www.johndoxey.100freemb.com/Silverwood/

The Coal Authority
coal.decc.gov.uk/

National Union of Mineworkers
num.org.uk

National Coal Museum for Wales
www.museumwales.ac.uk/bigpit

Mining History Network
projects.exeter.ac.uk/mhn/welcome.html

See also: 2.14 Wales, 4.19 Other Occupations and Apprentices

4.2 Police

The origins of policing date back to 1750, when chief magistrate Henry Fielding employed six officers from his offices in Bow Street – who became known as the Bow Street Runners. This was followed by the formation of the Marine Police (1798), Glasgow Police (1800) and London Metropolitan Police (1829). Survival of and access to police records varies from county to county, and some forces maintain their own museums and archives.

Essex Police Museum
essex.police.uk/museum/

Trawl indexes to officers in the Essex County Constabulary from the 1880s to the present day; these include officers who served in Colchester Borough Police (transferred to ECC in 1947) and Southend Borough Police (1914–69), plus reserves and female auxiliaries from the Second World War. Copies of service records can be ordered for £20.

British Transport Police History Group
btphg.org.uk

British Transport Police History Group has a blog-style homepage and various drop-down menus with news of its latest projects; research articles (go to History > Storybank); a photo gallery; lists of recipients of various honours, decorations and medals; plus a roll of honour.

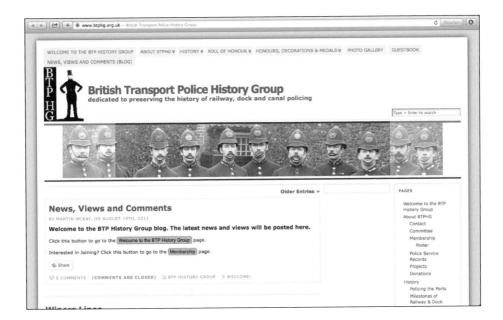

Staffordshire Name Indexes

www.staffsnameindexes.org.uk

Explore an index to Staffordshire Police Force Registers (1840–1920), plus a police disciplinary index (1857–86). If you're researching people from the other side of the fence, there's also a calendar of prisoners and an index to gaol inmate photographs.

Metropolitan Police Heritage Centre

metpolicehistory.co.uk

Research collections include a 54,000-name database from 1829 onwards, Central Records of Service from 1911, pension cards, Police Orders from 1857, Joiners and Leavers records (copies from The National Archives), and photographs.

Police Records Guide, The National Archives

nationalarchives.gov.uk/records/looking-for-person/policeofficer.htm

This is a guide to TNA's own police holdings, which relate to the Metropolitan Police, the Royal Irish Constabulary and the Transport Police. There are also two relevant podcasts available via the TNA's dedicated media section.

Police Records, Ancestry

ancestry.co.uk/cs/uk/criminal

Guide to Ancestry's criminal records collections, including police records from 1833 to 1914. These detail promotions, disciplinary actions, injuries, and even give physical descriptions.

History of the Met

content.met.police.uk/Site/history

Official history hub for the Met Police where you can follow a timeline, explore famous cases, and view sample records from the aforementioned Metropolitan Police Heritage Centre.

International Centre for the History of Crime, Policing and Justice

www.open.ac.uk/arts/research/policing/resources

The centre holds police-related journals, newsletters and articles, plus copies of Metropolitan police orders (1865–1950s). There's also a useful guide to regional police archives.

Manchester Police Index, Findmypast

search.findmypast.co.uk/search-world-records/manchester-police-index-1812-1941

Search 10,000+ records in the Manchester Police Index (1812–1941), which includes physical descriptions, religion/marital status, plus career history.

Kent Police Museum

kent-police-museum.co.uk

The museum offers a research service, including the personnel records of Kent police officers, from 1857 onwards, held at the Centre for Kentish Studies in Maidstone.

Police History Society

policehistorysociety.co.uk

A hub for experts in all areas of police history; handy for finding museums, special collections and local groups.

Metropolitan Women Police Association

metwpa.org.uk

Looks after records of service of women police officers from 1919 to 1986.

Lancashire Police

lancashire.gov.uk/education/record_office/records/policesearch.asp

Search officers from the Lancashire County Constabulary (1840–1925).

Police Roll of Honour Trust

policememorial.org.uk

Lists all UK police officers killed in the line of duty.

Metropolitan and City Police Orphans Fund

met-cityorphans.org.uk

Read about the world's oldest police charity.

Garda Síochána Historical Society

policehistory.com

Learn more about Ireland's national police.

Northern Ireland Police Museum

www.psni.police.uk/index/about-us/police_museum.htm

See also: 2.5 Crime and Punishment, 2.6 Court Records

4.3 Railways

If your ancestor was a railway worker prior to nationalization, then your first job will be to identify the region and company that employed them. And always keep in mind that the term 'rail worker' could cover a broad spectrum of occupations – from managers and clerks, to guards and porters, to engineers and drivers.

Railway Workers, Ancestry

ancestry.co.uk/cs/uk/occupations-alta

This is Ancestry's occupations page, from which you can find out more about the Railway Employment Records (1833–1956) collection, produced in association with TNA. The most common record type is the staff register, but there are also station transfers, and pension, accident, and apprentice records; you can browse the collection by company as well. Related collections here include *Great Western Railway Magazine* (1838–1943) and *Southern Railway Magazine* (1840–1942).

Modern Records Centre

www2.warwick.ac.uk/services/library/mrc/explorefurther/subject_guides/family_history/rail/

The University of Warwick's Modern Records Centre holds various trade union collections. This page describes rail unions, revealing which unions different workers were likely to join. For example, train drivers would normally join the Associated Society of Locomotive Engineers and Firemen, but a 'significant minority' were members of the National Union of Railwaymen. Clicking the union name leads to details of what records survive here.

Railway Staff Database, Cheshire

archives.cheshire.gov.uk/default.aspx?page=70

A database from Cheshire Archives, drawn from seventeen staff registers from four railway companies – Cambrian Railway, Great Western Railway, London and North Western Railway, and Great Western Joint Railway. The database contains about 25,000 names and stretches back to 1869. There's also a second database of employees of the railway works at Crewe (where Henry is given his new shape).

National Railway Museum
nrm.org.uk

Find out more about Search Engine – the NRM's library and archive. There's an online catalogue (hosted externally), PDF indexes to names in various staff magazines, and a list of railway websites compiled by NRM's librarian (delicious.com/Librarian_at_NRM). There's also a family history advice page at nrm.org.uk/NRM/ResearchAndArchive/researchhelp/FamilyHistory.

Railways Archive
railwaysarchive.co.uk

Gives access to key data and documents including the Beeching reports, an Accident Archive of nearly 9,000 incidents, a Document Archive and more.

Trade Union Ancestors
www.unionancestors.co.uk

Around 5,000 trade unions are known to have existed at one time or another, and tens of millions of people have been members.

Railway Ancestors
railwayancestors.org.uk

At the time of writing this useful website had disappeared. But you can still find archived versions by entering the address into archive.org's WayBack Machine.

Warwickshire Railways
warwickshirerailways.com

Histories of all the county companies, plus details of rail routes, stations, junctions, goods depots and more.

Transport Archives Register
trap.org.uk

Describes archives containing railway and canal records.

Science and Society Picture Library
ssplprints.com

Includes vast quantities of images from the National Railway Museum.

National Union of Railwaymen, 1913–2013
www2.warwick.ac.uk/services/library/mrc/explorefurther/images/nur/

An online exhibition commemorating the 100th anniversary of the union.

Single or Return, History of Transport Salaried Staffs' Association
tssa.org.uk/en/about-us/history/

Includes sections exploring the union during the First World War.

Railway Guide, National Records of Scotland
nrscotland.gov.uk/research/guides/railway-records

Includes photographs from railway company records in the image gallery.

Rail Map Online
railmaponline.com

Interactive map showing all past and present train routes.

British Steam
britishsteam.com

Illustrated compendium of steam locomotives.

ASLEF, The Train Drivers' Union
www.aslef.org.uk/information/100011/102822/history_of_aslef/

Railway Staff Guide, The National Archives
nationalarchives.gov.uk/records/research-guides/railway-staff.htm

Railway and Canal Historical Society
rchs.org.uk

London Transport Museum
ltmuseum.co.uk

GWR's Steam Museum
steam-museum.org.uk

Signal Box
signalbox.org

Irish Railway Record Society
www.irrs.ie

Great Western Railway Shareholders (1835–1932)
search.findmypast.co.uk/search-united-kingdom-records/gwr-shareholders

Midland Railway Society
midlandrailway.org.uk

Mike's Railway History
mikes.railhistory.railfan.net

See also: 4.11 Engineers and Manufacturing, 4.19 Other Occupations and Apprentices

4.4 Agricultural Labourers (Ag Labs)

If you're ready to move beyond the census and parish registers, you'll soon find that most ag labs didn't trouble the average record keeper. But there are potential places to find references to individuals, and lots of possible sources for finding out more about the wider rural community.

Museum of English Rural Life
reading.ac.uk/merl/

The museum looks after objects relating to all kinds of rural crafts and communities, including records of agricultural manufacturing firms, organizations and cooperatives, collections of personal records and journals of farm workers, and some farm accounts. The Archive and Museum Database is at reading.ac.uk/adlib/.

Old Maps Online
oldmapsonline.org

Maps can be wonderful sources: in this case for familiarizing yourself with the landscape your ancestor worked. This portal is a gateway to all kinds of historic maps, including tithe maps – accurate, large-scale charts, with corresponding tithe schedule books, that describe use, value, and names of owners/occupiers.

ConnectedHistories
connectedhistories.org

Federated search hub where you can trawl Victoria County History, which provides local histories of parishes and townships, sometimes detailing the fortunes and practices of individual farms. This comes from digital library British History Online (british-history.ac.uk).

Rural Museums Network

ruralmuseums.ssndevelopment.org

A quick and easy way to find individual rural museums dedicated to particular areas or crafts. Click on About Us > Members to find the complete list.

Foxearth and District Local History Society

foxearth.org.uk

Focuses on the border area between Essex and Suffolk, with photographs, postcards, oral histories, old maps, excerpts from newspapers and more.

Genuki Occupations

genuki.org.uk/big/Occupations.html

Gateway to all kinds of pages relating to different occupations.

Cynefin: A Sense of Place

cynefin.archiveswales.org.uk

Gives access to 1,200 sheets of Welsh tithe maps online.

Old Occupations

worldthroughthelens.com/family-history/old-occupations.php

A useful list if you ever stumble upon an unfamiliar occupation in the census.

ScotlandsPeople

scotlandspeople.gov.uk/content/help/index.aspx?r=551&430

Trawl more than 1,500 occupations, with definitions and variants.

National Museum of Rural Life, Scotland

nms.ac.uk/our_museums/museum_of_rural_life.aspx

Heritage Crafts Association

heritagecrafts.org.uk

Romany and Traveller Family History Society

rtfhs.org.uk

West Yorkshire Tithes

tracksintime.wyjs.org.uk

Vision of Britain

visionofbritain.org.uk

Ireland's Tithe Applotment Books

titheapplotmentbooks.nationalarchives.ie

See also: 1.3 The Census, 1.4 Parish Registers, 2.8 Poor Law and Workhouses, 2.23 Maps, 2.24 Estate Records, 3.4 Militia Men, 4.7 Rural Craftsmen

4.5 Merchant Navy

You'll find plenty of guidance for researching members of the merchant navy via the likes of the National Maritime Museum and The National Archives. There are also several important encyclopaedic amateur websites that can help you trace individual vessels.

Merchant Seaman Research Guide, The National Archives

nationalarchives.gov.uk/records/looking-for-person/merchantseaman1858-1917.htm

The Registrar General of Shipping and Seamen was responsible for keeping records of merchant seamen and so most material is held in the Board of Trade record series (BT). This particular guide focuses on tracing merchant seamen between 1858 and 1917, and has the usual live links to searchable sources available here and via external websites.

Maritime History Archive

www.mun.ca/mha/

Important Canadian archive that collects and preserves the history of maritime activities in the North Atlantic, and holds lots of material relating to British merchant shipping, including a large percentage of the surviving crew lists and agreements (1861–1913).

Register of Merchant Seamen, Southampton Archives

southampton.gov.uk/libraries-museums/local-family-history/southampton-archives/index-merchant-seamen.aspx

Information about the Central Index Register of Merchant Seamen, a collection of over a million merchant navy service record cards which can be accessed at Southampton Civic Archives reading room (or at TNA).

Medal Index, TNA Discovery

nationalarchives.gov.uk/records/merchant-seamen-medals-ww1.htm

From here you can search 155,000 index cards to the British War Medal, Mercantile Marine Medal and the Silver War Badge (1914–18). Discovery also has an Index of Apprentices at discovery.nationalarchives.gov.uk/details/r/C3188.

Crew List Index Project

crewlist.org.uk

CLIP has gathered a huge database of crew lists held in various archives. It is confined to merchant seafarers on British registered ships for the years 1861 to 1913 and the name index is also available via Findmypast.

Irish Mariners

irishmariners.ie

Details of over 23,000 Irish-born (and 1,000 Canadian-born) merchant seamen, contained in the CR10 series of central index cards held in the Southampton Civic Archives.

National Maritime Museum
rmg.co.uk/national-maritime-museum
Home to research guides, a fascinating collections section (collections.rmg.co.uk), plus catalogues to both the archive and library.

Lloyd's Marine Collection, Guildhall Library
guildhalllibrarynewsletter.wordpress.com/tag/lloyds-marine-collection/
Blog page describing the Lloyd's Marine Collection at the Guildhall Library. The parent website itself can be rather frustrating.

The Ships List
theshipslist.com
This site primarily hosts transcribed passenger lists but does include material that could be helpful when researching merchant shipping.

Welsh Mariners
welshmariners.org.uk
Includes an index of 23,500 Welsh merchant masters, mates and engineers active from 1800 to 1945.

Red Duster
red-duster.co.uk
Merchant Navy Association site with information about notable shipping companies and vessels.

Swansea Mariners
swanseamariners.org.uk
Transcribed information about merchant seaman on Swansea- and Cardiff-registered ships.

Merchant Navy, Wikipedia
en.wikipedia.org/wiki/British_Merchant_Navy
A concise introduction with pages on various shipping lines.

Merchant Marines, Genuki
genuki.org.uk/big/MerchantMarine.html
Useful list of merchant marine sources.

Mariners
mariners-l.co.uk
The website of the Mariners Mailing List.

Tracing Merchant Navy Ancestry, IWM
archive.iwm.org.uk/upload/pdf/famhistory_merchant2007.pdf

Port of London Authority Archive, Museum of London
museumoflondon.org.uk/collections-research/about-collections/port-london-authority-archive/

Merchant Navy Association
mna.org.uk

British Maritime History
www.barnettmaritime.co.uk

My Merchant Marines
mymerchantmarines.com

See also: 2.12 Migration, 2.13 Overseas Research, 3.2 Navy, 3.8 First World War, 3.9 Second World War, 3.12 Medals, 3.13 War Graves, 4.6 Fisherman and Whalers, 4.16 East India Company

4.6 Fishermen and Whalers

Maritime collections that might contain records of fishermen or whalers tend to survive in disparate archives and museums, meaning federated catalogues such as TNA's Discovery and Archives Wales come into their own. There are also local history websites that can tell you more about maritime communities and specific occupations, such as trawlermen, harbour masters or whalers.

Sailors' Families Society, Hull History Centre
hullhistorycentre.org.uk/discover/hull_history_centre/our_collections/source_guides/children's_homes_and_maternity.aspx

Via the catalogue you can search fishing records; records of shipping companies; 25,500 fishing crew lists for fishing vessels operating out of Hull between 1884 and 1914; and the likes of the Sailors' Children's Society.

Trinity House Maritime Museum
trinityhouseleith.org.uk

Traces its history back to 1380 when the shipowners and shipmasters of Leith set up a charitable foundation to assist destitute sailors and their families. Online galleries explore the history of Leith, the Trinity House building and the charity.

Grimsby Fishermen, North East Lincolnshire Archives
www.nelincs.gov.uk/faqs/archives-kept-north-east-lincolnshire-archives/

There is a searchable catalogue of collections which includes 38,000 Grimsby crew lists. The archives also look after registers of Grimsby ships (1824–1988) and registers of Grimsby fishing apprentices (1879–1937).

Hull Trawler
hulltrawler.net

Dedicated to Hull's fishing heritage, plus there are genealogy pages with databases collated from various sources, such as the census and local newspapers.

Scarborough Maritime Heritage Centre
scarboroughsmaritimeheritage.org.uk

Has photographs of fishermen and crews, plus articles on fishing families, which are arranged by surname.

National Maritime Museum
rmg.co.uk/national-maritime-museum

The research guides detail all kinds of potential sources such as *Olsen's Fisherman's Almanac*.

Brief History of Falmouth
falmouthport.co.uk/commercial/html/history.php

Example of a local history site, tracing the growth and development of the harbour and port.

Scotland's East Coast Fisheries
sites.scran.ac.uk/secf_final/index.php

Has sections on the herring industry, dangers at sea and arctic whaling.

Maritime History Archive
www.mun.ca/mha/
Another source for tracking down crew lists from 1863 to 1938.

Fishing History of Shetland
shetlopedia.com/Category:Fishing_History_of_Shetland

Crew List Index Project
crewlist.org.uk

Port of London Authority Archive
museumoflondon.org.uk/collections-research/about-collections/port-london-authority-archive/

True's Yard Fisherfolk Museum
www.truesyard.co.uk

Harbour Masters' Association
ukhma.org

Buckie and District Fishing Heritage Centre
buckieheritage.org

Scottish Maritime Museum
scottishmaritimemuseum.org

Scottish Fisheries Museum
scotfishmuseum.org

The Whaling Times
whalingtimes.com

Hunting the Whale: The History of Arctic Whaling from Eastern Scotland
historyshelf.org/secf/whale/

Whaling in Angus and Dundee
angusheritage.com/LocalHistoryCulture/IndustrialHeritage/Whaling.aspx

Polperro, Cornwall
polperro.org/fishing.html

See also: 4.5 Merchant Navy

4.7 Rural Craftsmen

The amount of surviving documentary evidence of cottage industries and rural crafts varies from place to place, and industry to industry. Local history collections held by libraries and museums may be your best bet for finding material relating to a rural community, although there are also several specialist websites that document the history of individual crafts.

Blacksmiths Index
blacksmiths.mygenwebs.com/

Ann Spiro's expanding Genealogical Index of Blacksmiths draws mainly from UK census material to record blacksmiths, plus related craftsmen such as cartwrights, wheelwrights, farriers and iron workers. The amount of detail on each craftsman varies, but as a minimum you can usually find name, birthdate, address and where the information came from.

Historical Directories
specialcollections.le.ac.uk/cdm/landingpage/collection/p16445coll4

Now available through the University of Leicester's Special Collections Online, here you can trawl for craftsmen and artisans in this free digital library of historic trade directories. Click the Find by Keywords button, enter an occupation, and narrow your search by location, decade or name.

Mills Archive
millsarchive.com

By far the most useful site for researching millers and millwrights. Run by the Mills Archive Trust it contains hundreds of images and documents, and the Mill People Database, which is derived from a variety of sources. Entries include the person's name, trade, place and notes, including the source.

Museum of English Rural Life
reading.ac.uk/merl/

You can explore photographic collections through the online image library, or browse archival material through the University of Reading's catalogue (reading.ac.uk/adlib/search/simple). The museum also looks after the Robert Dawson Romany Collection.

Lace Makers
cowperandnewtonmuseum.org.uk

The Cowper and Newton Museum is dedicated to William Cowper and his friend Rev. John Newton (who wrote 'Amazing Grace'). The website also has pages dedicated to the social history of the lace making trade – via the About Us drop-down menu.

Straw Plaiting in Hertfordshire

hertfordshire-genealogy.co.uk/data/occupations/straw-plait.htm

Hertfordshire Genealogy boasts over 10,000 pages and pictures about Old Hertfordshire, and these include several dedicated to the local straw plaiting industry.

Heritage Crafts Association

heritagecrafts.org.uk

Find out more about contemporary artisans still using traditional crafting techniques.

Genuki Occupations

genuki.org.uk/big/Occupations.html

Gateway to all kinds of pages relating to different occupations.

Old Occupations

worldthroughthelens.com/family-history/old-occupations.php

A useful list if you ever stumble upon an unfamiliar occupation in the census.

Rural Museums Network

ruralmuseums.ssndevelopment.org

Find rural museums dedicated to particular areas or crafts.

ScotlandsPeople

scotlandspeople.gov.uk/content/help/index.aspx?r=551&430

Trawl more than 1,500 occupations, with definitions and variants.

Romany and Traveller FHS

rtfhs.org.uk

National Wool Museum, Wales

museumwales.ac.uk/en/wool/

St Fagans Living Museum, Wales

museumwales.ac.uk/en/stfagans/living-museum/

Rural Life Centre, Surrey

rural-life.org.uk

National Museum of Rural Life, Scotland

nms.ac.uk/our_museums/museum_of_rural_life.aspx

British Agricultural History Society

bahs.org.uk

Sussex Mills Group

sussexmillsgroup.org.uk

Hampshire Mills Group
hampshiremills.org

Heron Corn Mill
heronmill.org

See also: 4.4 Agricultural Labourers, 4.6 Fishermen and Whalers, 4.19 Other Occupations and Apprentices

4.8 Teachers

Registers and log books that usually survive in school archives, and at local record offices, can be a goldmine for finding out about your ancestor's schooling, but also useful for researching the careers of teachers. Additionally, more and more universities offer online access to their digitized archives.

Teachers' Registration Records, Findmypast
search.findmypast.co.uk/search-united-kingdom-records/teachers-registration-council-registers-1914-1948

Contains details of just under 100,000 teachers registered with the Teachers' Registration Council (1914–48). When it was formed in 1914 the council recorded teachers already working, so it has some data going back to the 1870s. The amount of information varies, but includes name (and sometimes maiden name), date of registration, professional address, attainments, details of training and experience. The original registration records are with the Society of Genealogists (sog.org.uk).

University of Glasgow

universitystory.gla.ac.uk

Click University People and you can search records of 19,050 graduates up to 1914. Choose the more general People and you can search details of staff, lecturers and academics connected with the University. There are also First World War and Second World War rolls of honour – currently with 393 images, 400 biographies and 4,541 records of those who served.

British and Foreign School Society Archive

bfss.org.uk/archive/

Founded in 1808 to support free schools and teacher training. The archive, located at Brunel University, is fully catalogued; it holds data from the society's establishment onwards and includes papers of teacher training colleges associated with the BFSS – including Borough Road College, founded 1798, and Stockwell College.

National School Registers 1870–1914, Findmypast

findmypast.co.uk/school-registers

This resource launched in 2014 and expanded during 2015. It is the result of the National Digitisation Consortium, which has brought together 100+ archives and schools to contribute to the project. The registers date from between 1870 and 1914, and come from all over England and Wales. Although most users will be looking for pupils, teachers are also listed.

Institute of Education Archives, UCL

ioe.ac.uk/services/4389.html

Includes a PDF guide to archival collections held here, such as the College of Preceptors (later, the College of Teachers), established in 1846, which includes membership records; the Girls' Day School Trust (founded 1872); and the National Union of Women Teachers (founded 1904).

Teachers and Pupils Research Guide, The National Archives

nationalarchives.gov.uk/records/looking-for-person/teacher-or-pupil.htm

TNA doesn't hold any records of individual teachers or training colleges, but there is material about the administrative or policy files relating to teachers/teacher training in England and Wales.

Church of England Record Centre

lambethpalacelibrary.org/content/cerc

The centre has records of the National Society for Promoting Religious Education, established in 1811, which includes indexes of school teachers (1812–55).

Hidden Lives Revealed

hiddenlives.org.uk

Find details of homes run by the Children's Society (formerly the Waifs and Strays' Society) in late Victorian and early twentieth-century Britain.

Historical Directories of England and Wales
specialcollections.le.ac.uk/cdm/landingpage/collection/p16445coll4
Especially useful for checking the whereabouts of smaller schools.

Ragged School
maybole.org/history/articles/mayboleraggedschool.htm

See also: 2.9 Schools and Universities

4.9 Textile Workers

The textile industry was the powerhouse of the Industrial Revolution, and fed a global demand for high-quality materials from three main districts: the Midlands, the north-west of England, and the Clyde Valley in Scotland. Records of workers – and, more commonly, records of the firms that employed them – do survive, often in the form of factory wage books or union membership records.

Spinning the Web
spinningtheweb.org.uk

Dated but very useful site that brings together 20,000 documents – images, sound files and more – from the libraries, museums and archives across north-west England, to tell the story of the Lancashire cotton industry. It includes sections exploring the impact of cotton on villages, towns and cities, plus life for the people who lived and worked in the mills.

Textiles History, Archives Hub
archiveshub.ac.uk/features/textiles.shtml

The 2004 project Scottish Textile Heritage is no longer online. But you can find out more about some of the collections and partners via this page. You could also find archived versions of the original site by entering 'scottishtextileheritage.org.uk' into the Internet Archive's WayBack Machine (archive.org).

Cotton Town
cottontown.org

Again, slightly dated – but nevertheless informative – hub about the cotton industry in Blackburn and Darwen. You'll find lots of maps, manuscripts, photos, books, pamphlets and posters, with pages that touch on child labour, unrest, merchants and millowners, and working conditions.

Special Collections, University of Manchester Library
www.library.manchester.ac.uk/searchresources/guidetospecialcollections/atoz/

Search Special Collections for items such as the Oldham and Ashton Textile Employers' Association Archives. The library also has the *Cotton Factory Times*, which ran from 1885 to 1937, and included information on many individual millhands.

Scottish Textile Heritage Online

scottishtextileheritage.org.uk

Contains a searchable database of 3,000 descriptions of textile-related museum and archive collections and objects, along with a gallery of around 400 images.

Lancashire Cotton Cartoons

www.lancashirecottoncartoons.com

Features twentieth-century cartoons drawn by Sam Fitton, which appeared in the pages of the *Cotton Factory Times*.

New Lanark World Heritage Site

newlanark.org

Find out more about the settlement founded in 1786 by David Dale, who built cotton mills and housing for the mill workers.

Trade Union Ancestors

www.unionancestors.co.uk

Not specific to this industry, but useful research advice for tracking down records of trade unions.

Queen Street Textile Mill Museum, Burnley

lancashire.gov.uk/leisure-and-culture/museums/queen-street-mill-textile-museum.aspx

Boasts the only surviving nineteenth-century steam-powered weaving mill.

Working Class Movement Library
www.wcml.org.uk

Saltaire World Heritage Site
saltairevillage.info

Quarry Bank Mill
nationaltrust.org.uk/quarry-bank/

Manchester Cotton Mills
manchester2002-uk.com/history/victorian/mills.html

See also: 4.4 Agricultural Labourers, 4.7 Rural Crafts, 4.11 Engineers and Manufacturing, 4.19 Other Occupations and Apprentices

4.10 Doctors and Nurses

Before the National Health Service was established in 1948, health care for those unable to afford private treatment was provided either through charitable institutions such as hospitals and dispensaries, or local Poor Law authorities. For more information about researching the hospitals themselves, or their patients, see chapter 2.17.

Wellcome Trust
wellcome.ac.uk

Provides advice pages aimed at researching doctors, physicians, surgeons, apothecaries, nurses, midwives and dentists. It is currently working with a number of archives across the UK to digitize records of psychiatric hospitals dating back to the eighteenth century. Meanwhile, to begin delving into the vast Wellcome Library collections go to wellcomelibrary.org, where there are various online catalogues and digital highlights, such as this section relating to the Royal Army Medical Corps: wellcomelibrary.org/collections/digital-collections/royal-army-medical-corps/.

British Army Nurses' Service Records, The National Archives
nationalarchives.gov.uk/records/army-nurses-service-records.htm

Search and download First World War British Army Nurses' Service Records. These will tell you where a nurse trained, her references, and hospitals, field ambulances or other medical units where she served – and even what her superiors thought of her. Elsewhere, TNA also has research guides to health, hospitals, mental health and patients, doctors and nurses.

Royal College of Physicians, Munk's Roll
munksroll.rcplondon.ac.uk

Find out more about the Royal College of Physicians' Munk's Roll of Honour, a series of obituaries first compiled by Harveian librarian William Munk and published in 1861. Through this website you can search detailed, indexed biographies from eleven printed volumes covering the years 1518 to 2004.

British Optical Association Museum

college-optometrists.org/en/college/museyeum/

This site offers a free research service for family historians interested in opticians (optometrists) from the 1890s onwards. The site also has a few sample documents that show off the archives held here, including apprenticeship records.

Medical Museums

medicalmuseums.org

Useful A to Z of medical museums – from the Alexander Fleming Laboratory Museum to the Worshipful Society of Apothecaries. Click on Family History, and a list of museums with potential genealogical sources appear.

Lothian Health Services Archives

www.lhsa.lib.ed.ac.uk

The Family Historians page gives advice for those searching for records of a patient, nurse, doctor or other hospital employee.

Hospital Records Database

nationalarchives.gov.uk/hospitalrecords

Provides information about the location of the records of UK hospitals – currently over 2,800 entries.

Bethlem, Museum of the Mind

museumofthemind.org.uk

Find out more about the salary books and character books that can provide details about staff.

British Dental Association Museum

bda.org/museum

This site has an advice page and offers a research service for those tracing the careers of former dentists.

Lambeth Palace Library, Medical Licenses

lambethpalacelibrary.org

The library holds medical licenses issued by the Archbishops of Canterbury between 1535 and 1775.

Voluntary Hospitals Database

hospitalsdatabase.lshtm.ac.uk

A database maintained by the London School of Hygiene and Tropical Medicine.

Australian Medical Pioneers Index

medicalpioneers.com

Database of over 3,000 doctors from the 1700s through to 1875.

Clinical Notes

www.clinicalnotes.ac.uk

Searchable database of case notes dating back to the seventeenth century.

Royal College of Nursing, Library and Heritage Services

www.rcn.org.uk/development/library_and_heritage_services/library_services/genealogy_and_research_advice

Advice pages for genealogists.

Oxfordshire Health Archives

oxfordshirehealtharchives.nhs.uk

Fleming Museum

imperial.nhs.uk/aboutus/ourorganisation/museumsandarchives/index.htm

Royal British Nurses' Association

rbna.org.uk/archives.asp

Royal College of General Practitioners

www.rcgp.org.uk/about-us/history-heritage-and-archive/researching-a-medical-ancestor.aspx

Scarlet Finders, British Military Nurses

scarletfinders.co.uk

Royal College of Surgeons of Edinburgh, Library and Special Collections

www.library.rcsed.ac.uk/content/content.aspx

Edith Cavell
edithcavell.org.uk

Florence Nightingale Museum
www.florence-nightingale.co.uk

Army Medical Services Museum
ams-museum.org.uk / research.htm

See also: 2.17 Hospitals and Medicine

4.11 Engineers and Manufacturing

The records of heavy industry, engineering and manufacturing tend to survive in local record offices. Tyne and Wear Archives, for example, looks after archives of the shipbuilding trade that flourished in this part of the world – although, as is often the case, the records of the ships themselves are more comprehensive than the records of the workers who built them.

Modern Records Centre
www2.warwick.ac.uk / services / library / mrc /

The University of Warwick's Modern Records Centre holds motor industry records (especially relating to companies that formerly belonged to the Rover Group), records of trade associations, employers' organizations and related bodies, plus lots of useful information about individual trade unions and related organizations.

Trade Union Ancestors
www.unionancestors.co.uk

Around 5,000 trade unions are known to have existed at one time or another, and tens of millions of people have been members. This website aims to help family historians to identify the correct union, to discover the role their ancestor played in it, and to find out more about trade union history.

Electrical Engineers, Ancestry
ancestry.co.uk / cs / uk / occupations-alta

Landing page for key occupational records available via Ancestry, including Electrical Engineers (1871–1930) and Railway Workers (1833–1963). There are also Civil and Mechanical Engineer Records (1820–1930) that detail 100,000 names, plus Civil Engineer Photographs (1829–1923).

Tyne and Wear Archives
twmuseums.org.uk

Find out more about Tyne and Wear's archival holdings, including the internationally recognized shipbuilding collection. It also looks after mining records, many of which are catalogued and searchable online.

Institution of Civil Engineers

ice.org.uk/topics/historicalengineering/Archives

Read more about collections held here, including the genealogically useful application forms for all members who joined before 1930 (now available online through Ancestry). You can also search the ICE Image Library.

Institution of Mechanical Engineers

imeche.org/knowledge/library/archive

This site includes a searchable catalogue and details of the scope of its collections. There's a virtual archive section, picture gallery and a First World War roll of honour.

Historical Directories

specialcollections.le.ac.uk/cdm/landingpage/collection/p16445coll4

Search for references to manufacturing firms, engineers and other related trades and businesses through this free resource.

Institute of Mining Engineers, Durham Mining Museum

dmm.org.uk/mindex.htm

The Durham Mining Museum site includes lists of members of the North of England Institute of Mining Engineers, and a wide selection of transcribed documents.

Steam Engine Makers Database
www.geog.port.ac.uk/lifeline/sem_db/sem_db_home.html

This database contains information about members of early British trade union the Steam Engine Makers' Society, between 1835 and 1876.

Webster Signature Database Search Form
historydb.adlerplanetarium.org/signatures/

Repository for information preserved in collections worldwide about people who made scientific instruments.

Institution of Structural Engineers' Library
istructe.org/resources-centre/library

Looks after more than 60,000 publications covering all aspects of structural engineering.

Manufacturers, Genuki
genuki.org.uk/big/Occupations.html#Manufacturers

This is a limited list of pages relating to manufacturers.

Stan Cook's Gunmakers and Allied Trades Index
www.genuki.org.uk/big/Gunmakers.html

British Association of Paper Historians
baph.org.uk

North of England Institute of Mining and Mechanical Engineers Library
www.mininginstitute.org.uk

Sugar Refiners and Sugarbakers Database
www.mawer.clara.net/intro.html

See also: 4.1 Miners, 4.3 Railways, 4.19 Other Occupations and Apprentices

4.12 Bankers

Banks tend to be careful about their records, but the archives that survive are very spread out. The authors of *British Banking: A Guide to Historical Records* list more than 700 archive collections maintained by banks, county record offices, universities and local libraries.

ConnectedHistories
connectedhistories.org

A general 'banking' search of ConnectedHistories illustrates the kind of information you can uncover. One of 1,289 results from the Proceedings of the Old Bailey Online, for example, is the 1891 guilty plea from William Whyting, an employee of the London and County Banking Company who was accused of

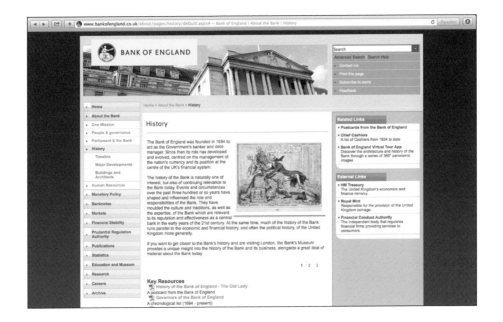

stealing £152 10s from his employers. Refine your search with the name 'Scott', and one of 3,996 results from British History Online is an excerpt from the House of Lords Journal, October 1831, which references Archibald Scott, an agent for the Leith Banking Company.

Bank of England History

bankofengland.co.uk/about/pages/history/default.aspx

General history of the bank with a virtual tour app, a list of chief cashiers from 1694 to date, plus details of banknotes, archives and the museum. There are various digitized sources (including Court of Directors' Minutes 1694–1913), a Flickr stream (flickr.com/photos/bankofengland/), plus a War Gallery showing the memorial to staff killed in both world wars.

RBS Heritage Hub

heritagearchives.rbs.com/use-our-archives/your-research/british-banking-history.html

Contains information about all British and Irish banks that became part of RBS, including an overview of archives which you can browse alphabetically or geographically. If you're interested in the origins of UK banking then there's a page dedicated to Cheapside goldsmith Edward Backwell, one of the first men to make banking his primary trade.

Lloyds Archives

lloydsbankinggroup.com/our-group/our-heritage/our-archives/

This site includes details of staff records (registers, salary records) and the harder to find customer records (account ledgers) preserved in the archives, plus information about how to make an enquiry or sample the records yourself. There's also a complete collections index.

Gurney Family Banking in Norwich

heritagecity.org/research-centre/industrial-innovation/the-gurney-family-and-banking-in-norwich.htm

Page describing the history of a Quaker family bank, started in Norwich, which would eventually become part of Barclays Bank.

Business Records Guide, The National Archives

nationalarchives.gov.uk/records/looking-for-subject/business.htm

Two useful TNA guides include this example, which relates to business records held in the UK, and the associated guide, Companies and Businesses: Further Research.

HSBC Archives

hsbc.com/about-hsbc/company-history/hsbc-archives

Describes HSBC's archives, which also contain records of banks acquired by HSBC (and its predecessor companies). Includes a video tour of the archives.

Coutts History

coutts.com/about-us/history/

One of the world's oldest banks – founded in 1692 by Scottish goldsmith-banker John Campbell.

Banking in Essex

essex-family-history.co.uk/banking.htm

Short article describing the emergence of organized banking in Essex 'before the coming of Barclays'.

C. Hoare and Co.

hoaresbank.co.uk/our-history

Private bankers since 1672. This history section includes a timeline and manuscript of the month.

Banking Ancestors, WDYTYA? Magazine

whodoyouthinkyouaremagazine.com/tutorials/jobs/banking-ancestors

Tutorial on researching banking ancestors from regular contributor Jenny Thomas.

Rothschild History

rothschild.com/our_history/

Read about the rise of the Rothschilds in the early nineteenth century.

4.13 Lawyers

Law was the first profession to have a regularly published list of its practitioners. This began with the likes of the annual *Browne's General Law List* (starting 1775), which became the *New Law List* and then simply the *Law List*.

Lincoln's Inn Archives

lincolnsinn.org.uk/index.php/library/the-inns-archives

The archive of the Honourable Society of Lincoln's Inn – one of four Inns of Court in London to which barristers of England and Wales belong and where they are called to the Bar. These hold the longest-running record series of any of the four Inns. The so-called Black Books commenced in 1422 and were essentially memoranda books of business.

Law Society Corporate Archive

lawsociety.org.uk/support-services/library-services/corporate-archive/

Holds the Law Society's corporate archive collection dating back to the beginning of the society in 1825. The society's library catalogue is at wv-tls.hostedbyfdi.net/webview/. Law Society research guides are at lawsociety.org.uk/support-services/library-services/research-guides/, and include 'How to trace past solicitors'.

Gray's Inn Archives

graysinn.org.uk/history/archives

The oldest and most complete series is the collection of Pension Books – records of the meetings of the Inn's governing body beginning in 1569. The site also provides links to external digitized transcriptions of both the Pension Books and Register of Admissions.

Lawyer Research Guide, The National Archives

nationalarchives.gov.uk/records/looking-for-person/lawyer.htm

Complete guide which details sources available online. You can, for example, search articles of clerkship using the name of the qualified solicitor, or the person they were training, through the advanced search option in Discovery.

Middle Temple Archives

middletemple.org.uk/about-us/history/

This is the general history section of the website, which also links to the archive pages. Online sources include the Register of Admissions (from the fifteenth century to 1944) and Middle Temple Records: Minutes of Parliament (1501–1703).

Inner Temple Admissions Database

innertemple.org.uk/history/the-archives

Details of the Inner Temple archives, including the free Admissions Database (1547–1920), which has biographical information about past members of the Honourable Society of the Inner Temple.

Law Society's Solicitors Regulation Authority

sra.org.uk

The Law Society maintains a register listing lawyers admitted since 1845 (back to 1790 for most courts), plus some Registers of Articles of Clerkship since 1860.

Lawyers in England and Wales Wiki, FamilySearch

familysearch.org/learn/wiki/en/Lawyers_in_England_and_Wales

Excellent summary of the profession, listing potential sources and online data.

Register of Admissions to Gray's Inn, 1521–1889

archive.org/details/registerofadmiss00gray

Free digitized copy, via archive.org.

Institute of Advanced Legal Studies, University of London

ials.sas.ac.uk/library/archives/rlea.htm

4.14 Clergy

Although the word 'clergy' might be used to describe leaders from any religion, in this instance the focus is clergy who operated in Christian denominations in the United Kingdom, and the websites that can help genealogists find out more about their lives and careers.

Clergy of the Church of England Database

theclergydatabase.org.uk

This database brings together biographical data of clergymen between 1540 and 1835. There is information on dioceses, lists of bishops and locations where clergy served. An upgrade in 2014 brought new data for the diocese of Canterbury since 1780, new material for the diocese of London, plus material about posts overseas.

The Cause Papers Database

hrionline.ac.uk/causepapers/

Searchable catalogue of more than 14,000 cause papers relating to cases heard between 1300 and 1858 in the Church Courts of the diocese of York. The original records are held in the Borthwick Institute for Archives, and cover a wide variety of cases including breaches of faith by clergy.

Crockford's Clerical Directory

www.crockford.org.uk

The online edition of *Crockford's Clerical Directory* contains biographical details of more than 27,000 Anglican clergy. The book was first published in 1858, although here you can only explore data going back to 1968, which was the first time the information was put into electronic form.

Church of England Collection, Lambeth Palace Library

lambethpalacelibrary.org

The historic library of the Archbishops of Canterbury and the principal library and record office for the history of the Church of England. You can also find contact details for the Church of England Record Centre, whose core collections date from 1704.

American Emigrant Ministers 1690–1811, Ancestry

search.ancestry.co.uk/search/db.aspx?dbid=4760

This site lists clergy who received funds from the English crown for passage to the Americas. It is one of several relevant sources on Ancestry – others include the Clergy List of 1897 (search.ancestry.co.uk/search/db.aspx?dbid=34776).

British History Online

british-history.ac.uk

Click on Subject and the drop-down menu includes ecclesiastical and religious history. The resulting list includes digitized copies of higher CofE clergy between 1066 and 1857.

Methodist Ministers

www.library.manchester.ac.uk/searchresources/guidetospecialcollections/ methodist/using/indexofministers/

Online index of Methodist ministers which is maintained by the University of Manchester's John Rylands Library (manchester.ac.uk/library/rylands).

Clergy Sources, FamilyRelatives

familyrelatives.com

Under Trade and Occupational you will find data drawn from Crockford's, Clergy Lists and the Catholic Directory for the Clergy and Laity in Scotland.

E 179 Database

apps.nationalarchives.gov.uk/e179/

Database contains descriptions of every document in series E 179 relating to the taxation of the laity in England and Wales.

Looking for Records of Clergy, The National Archives

nationalarchives.gov.uk/records/looking-for-person/clergy.htm

Tracing Clergy and Lay Persons, Guildhall Library

www.history.ac.uk/gh/clergy.htm

See also: 1.4 Parish Registers, 2.18 Catholic, 2.20 Nonconformist

4.15 Coastguard and Customs

In section 2 there is information about how to find records of taxation. Here we turn to the individuals involved in the mechanics of the tax system, and the customs and excise men who enforced it.

Customs and Coastguard Guides, The National Archives

nationalarchives.gov.uk/records/looking-for-person/customs-officer.htm

Before starting research into a customs or excise man, you need to attempt to find out the county in which they were posted and the dates of service. You can browse Customs Board Minute Books (1734–1885) via Discovery, which may record transfers, suspensions, resignations and pensions for officers. This page also has links to the related guide to Excise Officers and the Coastguard, plus you can browse and download Coastguard Establishment Books and Registers (1816–1947) for free.

HM Waterguard

hm-waterguard.org.uk

Dedicated to the history, men and work of the Preventive Service of HM Customs and Excise. It includes details of uniform, including badges, caps, buttons and insignia, pay and working conditions, training, plus photos and video clips, anecdotes and memories from the various divisions. You can download and read PDF copies of the union magazine *The Customs Journal*.

Scottish Customs and Excise Records Guide, National Records of Scotland

nrscotland.gov.uk/research/guides/customs-and-excise-records

Concise guide to surviving records of customs staff, excise staff (many records were lost in a fire in the nineteenth century) and shipping registers; the site also lists customs and excise records held elsewhere.

Parliamentary Papers
parlipapers.chadwyck.co.uk/marketing/index.jsp

Consult Parliamentary Papers for published reports of customs activities. They can be searched online, but only from subscribing organizations.

Mariners
mariners-l.co.uk/UKCustoms.html

A short piece on customs and excise men from the website of the Mariners Mailing List.

Merseyside Maritime Museum
liverpoolmuseums.org.uk/maritime/archive/sheet/44

Guide to tracing your ancestors who worked in HM Customs and Excise.

Coastguards of Yesteryear
coastguardsofyesteryear.org

Includes articles, photos, research guides and a modest records database.

Coastguards, Genuki
genuki.org.uk/big/Coastguards

List of coastguard officers with dates and places of birth.

Naval Medal and Award Rolls, Ancestry
search.ancestry.co.uk/search/db.aspx?dbid=1687

Browse First World War campaign medals for coastguards.

Customs Collector
customscollector.com

Site aimed at collectors of customs insignia.

The Courtney Library, Royal Cornwall Museum
www.royalcornwallmuseum.org.uk/courtney-library/

Border Force National Museum
liverpoolmuseums.org.uk/maritime/visit/floor-plan/seized/

Cornwall Record Office, HM Customs and Excise Outport Shipping Registers
cornwall.gov.uk/community-and-living/records-archives-and-cornish-studies/cornwall-record-office/cornwall-record-office-collections/public-records/hm-customs-and-excise-outport-shipping-registers/

Smugglers and Smuggling in Cornwall
cornwall-calling.co.uk/smugglers.htm

Smugglers' Britain
smuggling.co.uk

See also: 2.3 Taxation, 4.5 Merchant Navy, 4.6 Fisherman and Whalers

4.16 East India Company

The East India Company played a vital role in British expansion and control overseas. For hundreds of years it employed thousands of traders, administrators, politicians, sailors and soldiers. The company established the first British outpost in South Asia in 1619 at Surat on the north-western coast, and at its height it is estimated that it accounted for half of the world's trade.

Families in British India Society
fibis.org

While parts of FIBIS are only open to members, there is still plenty of very useful and freely available material here, including a searchable database of more than 1,411,000 individual names. Recent additions include letters from residents to Governor-General Lord Canning, around the time of the Indian Mutiny.

FIBIS Wiki
wiki.fibis.org/index.php/East_India_Company

Following on from the above, the FIBIS wiki is packed with useful information for researchers, including this page dedicated to the East India Company. There are related articles on the company's factories and army, associated Acts of Parliament, plus various occupations.

India Office, Family History Search
indiafamily.bl.uk/ui/home.aspx

Official BL sub-site where you can search 300,000 births, baptisms, marriages, deaths and burials in the India Office Records, which mainly document British and European people in India (*c*.1600–1949). There's also the India Office Help For Researchers page at bl.uk/reshelp/findhelpregion/asia/india/indiaoffice records/indiaofficehub.html.

East India Company Ships
eicships.info/index.html

Aims to provide information on ships and voyages of the East India Company's mercantile service, including details of the vessels (construction details, owners), voyages (dates, ports, crew) and more.

British India Office Collection, Findmypast
findmypast.co.uk/articles/world-records/search-all-uk-records/special-collections/british-india-office-collection

Findmypast collection, through partnership with the BL, where you can find BMD material plus military/naval pensions, wills, estate papers, marriage notifications and more.

East India Company and Asia, National Maritime Museum
rmg.co.uk/whats-on/exhibitions/traders

Explore permanent museum gallery 'Traders: the East India Company and Asia', which focuses on 250 years of trading.

East India Company
theeastindiacompany.com

The official company website.

East India Company Research Guide, Royal Museums Greenwich
rmg.co.uk/researchers/library/research-guides/shipping-companies/research-guide-f5-the-east-india-company

East India Company at Home, UCL Research Blog
blogs.ucl.ac.uk/eicah/

Records of British Colonies and Dependencies Guide, The National Archives
nationalarchives.gov.uk/records/looking-for-place/coloniesanddependencies.htm

Indian Cemeteries
indian-cemeteries.org

See also: 2.12 Migration, 2.13 Overseas Research, 4.5 Merchant Navy

4.17 Brewers and Publicans

Sources for researching members of the brewing industry or publicans include applications for permission to keep an alehouse, pledges to operate orderly pubs, trade and street directories, and brewery staff records.

Pub History Society

pubhistorysociety.co.uk

Special interest society, established in 2001, where you can find useful links, interesting news stories, material relating to historic pubs and inns, pub signs, drinking vessels, traditional pub games and more. There's also a downloadable guide to tracing your publican ancestors.

Pubs History

pubshistory.com

A host of useful data taken from a variety of sources, mostly concentrating on the south of England, but gradually moving north. Highlights include an index of London pubs from 1944; London pubs, beer retailers and hotels taken from a post office directory from 1899; and a directory of Sheffield pubs.

Brewery History Society

breweryhistory.com

Under the Heritage menu there's a gazetteer of pre-1940 breweries operating in England. There are also details of the society's archive (held in various repositories) and a pictorial database of pub and brewery buildings that still display advertising for now-defunct breweries.

Guinness Archive Index

guinness-storehouse.com/en/genealogysearch.aspx

Also searchable via Ancestry, this is the official Guinness Archive index that records some 20,000 employees of the St James Brewery in Dublin going back as far as 1759. You can search for employees by name, date of birth and year of employment.

Brewers' Hall

www.brewershall.co.uk/history-and-treasures/

History of the livery company which, unlike most of the ancient livery companies, has remained close to its trade, and boasts some of the oldest continuous records in the memorandum book of William Proland, company clerk from 1418–40.

Scottish Brewing Archive

archives.gla.ac.uk/sba/default.html

The Scottish Brewing Archive at the University of Glasgow has records, advertisements and ephemera. There's an alphabetical list of breweries and associated firms whose records are held here.

Victuallers Database, Warwickshire County Record Office

apps.warwickshire.gov.uk/Victuallersdb/victuallers/indexes

Details of licensed victuallers in Warwickshire between 1801 and 1828, searchable by parish, victualler, pub name, year or bondsman's surname.

Warwick Modern Records Centre
www2.warwick.ac.uk/services/library/mrc/

The centre preserves the Brewers' Society archive, which includes bound sets of *Brewing Trade Review* and artwork for advertising campaigns.

Building History
buildinghistory.org

Full of useful research tips if you're trying to find out more about the brewery building or pub where your ancestor worked.

Surrey Licensed Victuallers, Ancestry
search.ancestry.co.uk/search/db.aspx?dbid=4835

Search registers of licensed victuallers between 1785 and 1903, from material held at the Surrey History Centre.

Beer in the Evening
beerintheevening.com

Modern review site with details of some 43,500 venues across the UK.

Historical Directories
specialcollections.le.ac.uk/cdm/landingpage/collection/p16445coll4

Search for pubs, breweries and related trades/firms.

National Brewing Library
brookes.ac.uk/library/speccoll/brewing.html

Part of Special Collections at Oxford Brookes University.

Publican and Brewery Records, GenGuide
genguide.co.uk/source/publican-brewery-and-licensed-victuallers-records-occupations/127/

Pubs and Inns, Archives Hub
archiveshub.ac.uk/features/pubsandinns.shtml.

Campaign for Real Ale
camra.org.uk

Heritage Pubs
www.heritagepubs.org.uk

Pubs in Hull and East Yorkshire
paul-gibson.com/pubs-and-breweries/beverley-pubs-k-to-l.php#

Lost Pubs Project
closedpubs.co.uk

Inn Sign Society
innsignsociety.com

Beamish Museum
beamish.org.uk

A Story to Tell – Scotland's Pubs and Bars
scotlandspubsandbars.co.uk

History of Advertising Trust
hatads.org.uk

4.18 Entertainers

If your ancestor crept the boards or perhaps spent time as a professional musician, you are most likely to find references to their work via local record offices, specialist archives or perhaps a venue's own collection. In particular, the history of music hall is a very popular subject, with lots of background material online.

The Stage Archive
archive.thestage.co.uk

The Stage was founded by Maurice Comerford and Lionel Carson in February 1880 as a monthly newspaper. This archive of more than 6,500 issues contains previews/reviews, plus details of actors, theatres and performances. Advanced options allow searches by articles, pictures or advertisements. Searches are free, while viewing results costs £5 (24-hour pass) to £150 (annual access).

National Fairground Archive
shef.ac.uk/nfa

The NFA focuses on transient fairground performers, and there's a digital portal section with images, ephemera, maps and plans, plus moving images and sound files. The Research and Articles section leads to hyperlinked themes covering the likes of fairs, circuses, magic, variety and early cinema, and detailing relevant NFA holdings

Playbills of the Theatre Royal Edinburgh, National Library of Scotland
digital.nls.uk/playbills/

There are an estimated 10,000 playbills held in the National Library of Scotland. Here you can browse examples from the Theatre Royal Edinburgh and see who performed in a particular play. There's also a collection of 8,713 theatre programmes at nls.uk/collections/british/theatres/index.cfm.

East London Theatre Archive
www.elta-project.org/

Image database of ephemera from collections held by the V&A, individual theatres, plus the UEL (University of East London) archives. You can search the content by theatre, time, subject or name, and then click and zoom in on individual playbills, programmes, press cuttings and photographs.

Theatre Collection, University of Bristol

bris.ac.uk/theatrecollection/

There's an online catalogue where you can search for actors, directors, designers, composers and playwrights, and results include details of performances and catalogue records.

British Newspaper Archive

britishnewspaperarchive.co.uk

Search for references in national and regional papers, or the likes of defunct weekly title *The Era* – known in its day as the 'actor's bible' – which includes advertisements, reviews and performances.

Theatrical Scenery

theatrical-scenery.info

This site's content is based on the private archive of set builders Brunskill and Loveday; it has a database of twentieth-century productions with free-to-view images of programmes, scenery and actors.

Footlight Notes

footlightnotes.tripod.com/index.html

Dated website with images of performers from variety theatre, music hall, vaudeville, circus, opera and ballet, plus reviews and biographical details.

Arthur Lloyd

arthurlloyd.co.uk

Music hall site inspired by popular performer Arthur Lloyd (1839–1904). Includes an illustrated database of London's Lost Theatres.

Scottish Theatre Archive

gla.ac.uk/services/specialcollections/collectionsa-z/scottishtheatrearchive/

Collections include programmes, scripts, production notes, photographs, posters and press cuttings.

London Music Hall Database

royalholloway.ac.uk/drama/Music-hall/index.asp

Sample database of 9,386 entries drawn from advertisements printed in *The Era* between 1865 and 1890.

Association of Performing Arts Collections

performingartscollections.org.uk/resources/

Hosts a general UK Theatre Collections database, with descriptions of over 250 collections.

Theatre and Performance, V&A

vam.ac.uk/collections/theatre_performance/

Details of the V&A's Theatre and Performance collections, founded in the 1920s.

Royal College of Music Library and Archive
rcm.ac.uk/library/contactus/archivesandrecords/
Preserves 600,000 concert programmes dating back to 1730.

Alhambra Theatre, Bradford, West Yorkshire Archives Service
wyorksarchivestreasures.weebly.com/the-alhambra-theatre.html
An example of the kind of material that might survive at your local record office.

British Music Hall Society
britishmusichallsociety.com
'We are a bunch of mad keen fans of music hall and variety …'

London Symphony Orchestra Archive
lso.co.uk/about-the-lso-archive
Preserves a collection of programmes dating from 1904.

Scottish Music Hall and Theatre Society
scottishmusichallsociety.webs.com

National Brass Band Archive
nationalbrassbandarchive.com

D'Oyly Carte Opera Company Archive
doylycarte.org.uk/archive

The Lamb Collection – Entertainment in the Nineteenth Century
sites.scran.ac.uk/lamb/entertain.htm

Musicians' Union
musiciansunion.org.uk

4.19 Other Occupations and Apprentices

Below are a hotchpotch of general resources that are useful for researching occupations and apprentices, plus some of the more impressive online archives retained by existing firms and industry bodies.

Modern Records Centre
www2.warwick.ac.uk/services/library/mrc/explorefurther/subject_guides/family_history/

The centre appears several times within these pages, thanks partly to its unrivalled collection of trade union archives. It also has this very useful introductory page aimed at family historians – a list of commonly searched trades/occupations, adapted from a 1927 dictionary produced by the Ministry of Labour. Each trade/occupation links to more detailed information about the unions associated with it, and the genealogical sources held at the centre. Some digitized union material held here is available via Findmypast.

London Apprenticeship Abstracts (1442–1850), Findmypast
search.findmypast.co.uk/search-world-records/london-apprenticeship-abstracts-1442-1850

Findmypast's Apprenticeship Abstracts formerly available on Origins.net and drawn from various London livery companies. There's also the Findmypast Occupations page (findmypast.co.uk/articles/world-records/search-all-uk-records/education-and-work/occupations) which leads to collections such as Thames Watermen and Lightermen (1688–2010) and the *Dental Surgeons Directory* (1925).

Working Class Movement Library
www.wcml.org.uk

The Salford-based library documents the 'labour movement, its allies and its enemies' since the eighteenth century. The online catalogue contains details of archival material such as trade union records, personal papers and records of organizations – and there's a family history section.

National Records of Scotland
nrscotland.gov.uk/research/visit-us/scotlandspeople-centre/useful-websites-for-family-history-research/occupations

Limited but still useful list of sites relating to various occupations. There's also a hyperlink to the NRS's own occupation research guides, such as this example relating to shipbuilding: nrscotland.gov.uk/research/guides/shipbuilding-records.

Occupations and Education, Ancestry
ancestry.co.uk/cs/uk/occupations-alta

The Occupations page leads to several unique collections not available elsewhere, such as British Postal Service Appointment Books (1737–1969), Civil Engineer Lists (1818–1930) and Electrical Engineer Lists (1871–1930). There are also videos with advice and tips tailored to occupations research.

British Telecom Digital Archives
www.digitalarchives.bt.com

This website doesn't actually work very well, but there are various searchable resources, including almost half a million photographs, reports and items of correspondence from the archives, going back to 1846.

Companies Registration Office Records (1844–1980), The National Archives
nationalarchives.gov.uk/records/looking-for-subject/business.htm

Search the Companies Registration Office Records (BT 31 and BT 41) for information about the registration/dissolution of companies between 1844 and 1980. These records include registered companies only and are not the records of the companies themselves.

Union History

unionhistory.info

TUC history online has sections on the General Strike, match workers, and the impact of 1914 novel *The Ragged Trousered Philanthropists* – plus you can explore a completely digitized version of an original manuscript. There's also a useful links section.

Scottish Archive of Print and Publishing History Records

sapphire.ac.uk

Lots of fascinating content including 'Papermaking on the Water of Leith' and sections on pre- and post-Industrial Revolution papermaking. The records include a 'substantial oral history archive and database'.

John Lewis Memory Store

johnlewismemorystore.org.uk

Site bringing together memories and photos of working life at the John Lewis Partnership. You can find out more about the archive itself at johnlewis partnership.co.uk/about/our-history/archives-collection.html.

Trade Union Ancestors

www.unionancestors.co.uk

Some useful information for tracing members of a union. Plus there's the fascinating sister site which explores the history of the Chartist Movement at chartists.net.

Woolworths Museum

woolworthsmuseum.co.uk

Virtual museum which tells the story of Woolworths from its birth in Lancaster, PA, and boasts various letters, documents and ephemera from the archive.

The Sainsbury Archive, Museum of London

archive.museumoflondon.org.uk/sainsburyarchive/

Home to more than 16,000 documents, photographs and objects tracing the history of the supermarket since the first shop opened in 1869.

Apprentices and Masters Guide, The National Archives

nationalarchives.gov.uk/records/looking-for-person/apprentice.htm

Other useful guides include People in Business and Trades (nationalarchives. gov.uk/records/looking-for-person/other-occupations.htm).

Apprenticeship of Workhouse Children, Workhouses.org

workhouses.org.uk/education/apprenticeship.shtml

This part of the Children and Education section on the wonderful Workhouses.org website details the workings of the apprenticeship system.

Frogmore Paper Mill
thepapertrail.org.uk
Online home of the working Frogmore Paper Mill in Hemel Hempstead –
'Birthplace of Paper's Industrial Revolution.'

Guildhall Library
cityoflondon.gov.uk/things-to-do/visiting-the-city/archives-and-city-history/
guildhall-library/Pages/default.aspx
Find out about the Guildhall Library's important collections of apprenticeship and
other occupational records.

Save the Wedgwood Collections
savewedgwood.org
Read about the successful campaign to save the Wedgwood Museum's historic
archive collections (wedgwoodmuseum.org.uk).

Street Directories, PRONI
streetdirectories.proni.gov.uk
Explore street directories from Belfast, and surrounding towns, which span much
of the nineteenth century.

I Worked at Raleigh
iworkedatraleigh.com
Home to video clips, stories, photographs, and more, relating to working life at
the bicycle factory in Nottingham.

Design Collection, The National Archives
design.nationalarchives.gov.uk
The National Archives holds the records of almost 3 million designs dating from
1839 to 1991.

Historical Directories
specialcollections.le.ac.uk/cdm/landingpage/collection/p16445coll4/hd/
Digital library of local and trade directories for England and Wales (1750–1919).

Sussex Record Society
sussexrecordsociety.org
Among the society's free-to-view online books is *Sussex Apprentices & Masters
(1710–52)*.

Scottish Printing Archival Trust
scottishprintarchive.org
'Records, preserves and shares Scotland's printing heritage.'

LiveryCompanies
liverycompanies.com
Database of the livery companies of the City of London.

Occupations, Scottish Archive Network
scan.org.uk/familyhistory/myancestor/index.htm

Dictionary of Scottish Architects
scottisharchitects.org.uk

Occupations, Genuki
genuki.org.uk/big/Occupations.html

Business Archives Council of Scotland
www.gla.ac.uk/services/archives/bacs/

Researching Occupations, TheGenealogist
thegenealogist.co.uk/featuredarticles/2012/discover-the-working-history-of-your-ancestors-50/

Trade Union Membership Registers, Findmypast
search.findmypast.co.uk/search-world-records/britain-trade-union-membership-registers

Register of Duties Paid for Apprentices' Indentures (1710–1811), Ancestry
search.ancestry.co.uk/search/db.aspx?dbid=1851

Museum of Childhood
vam.ac.uk/moc/

England Occupations, FamilySearch Wiki
familysearch.org/learn/wiki/en/England_Occupations

Old Occupations in Scotland
scotsfamily.com/occupations.htm

People's History Museum, Labour History Archive and Study Centre
phm.org.uk/archive-study-centre/

Working Lives Research Institute
workinglives.org

Tolpuddle Martyrs' Museum
tolpuddlemartyrs.org.uk

New Lanark World Heritage Site
newlanark.org

Working Life, Celebrated in Photographs
workinglife.org.uk

Marks and Spencer Company Archive
marksintime.marksandspencer.com

Section 5

MISCELLANEOUS

5.1 Resources by Region

This is a list of archival and society websites by region. Some are little more than holding pages with collection descriptions and contact details. Others have huge amounts of digital finding aids, research guides, image libraries and more.

NATIONAL

British Library
bl.uk

The National Archives
nationalarchives.gov.uk

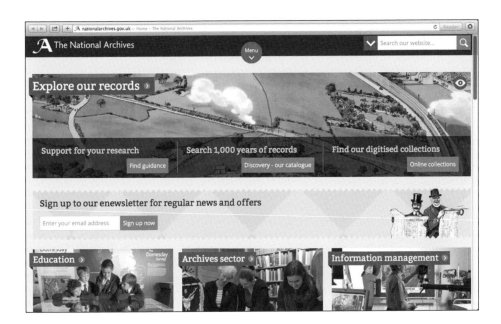

The National Archives of Ireland
nationalarchives.ie

The National Library of Wales
llgc.org.uk

The National Records of Scotland
nrscotland.gov.uk

Public Record Office of Northern Ireland
www.proni.gov.uk

Find An Archive, The National Archives
discovery.nationalarchives.gov.uk

Formerly available through The National Archives' Archon Directory, you can now search the register of 2,500 archives through the Discovery page. Scroll down to the Find an Archive box to begin. Other useful bodies include Archives Wales (archiveswales.org.uk), the Scottish Archive Network (scan.org.uk) and AIM25 (aim25.ac.uk).

Find a Society, Federation of Family History Societies
ffhs.org.uk/members2/contacting.php

This is the Federation of Family History Societies' list of member groups, covering all of the UK, some overseas societies, a handful of one-name studies groups and 'other'. There's also the Scottish Association of FHS's list of members at: safhs.org.uk/members.asp.

REGIONAL: ENGLAND

Bedfordshire

Bedfordshire and Luton Archives
bedfordshire.gov.uk/archive/

Has a free Bedfordshire Gaol Register database (apps.bedfordshire.gov.uk/grd/) and an online catalogue.

Bedfordshire FHS
bfhs.org.uk

Berkshire

Berkshire Record Office
berkshirerecordoffice.org.uk

The Office holds probate records from 1480 to 1857 and a 39,000-name index is available on CD. There are also sections exploring the history of Victorian Broadmoor and Fair Mile Hospital.

Berkshire FHS
berksfhs.org.uk

Buckinghamshire

Centre for Buckinghamshire Studies
www.buckscc.gov.uk/leisure-and-culture/centre-for-buckinghamshire-studies/
The homepage has signposts to historic photographs, including Victorian prisoners, plus a Buy Online page where you can order copies of wills and parish register entries, while in Online Resources there are trade directories, maps, and the Bombs over Bucks census of Second World War bomb sites.

Buckinghamshire FHS
bucksfhs.org.uk

Bristol and Avon

Bristol Record Office
bristolmuseums.org.uk/bristol-record-office/

Bristol and Avon FHS
bafhs.org.uk

Cambridgeshire

Cambridgeshire Archives
www.cambridgeshire.gov.uk/info/20011/archives_archaeology_and_museums/177/archives_and_local_studies
There's also a free BMD search facility at Camdex: camdex.org.

Cambridgeshire FHS
cfhs.org.uk

Cambridgeshire Records Society
cambsrecordsociety.co.uk

Cheshire

Cheshire Archives and Local Studies
archives.cheshire.gov.uk

Family History Society of Cheshire
fhsc.org.uk

Cornwall

Cornwall Record Office
cornwall.gov.uk/community-and-living/records-archives-and-cornish-studies/

Cornwall FHS
cornwallfhs.com

Cumbria

Cumbria Archives Service
cumbria.gov.uk/archives/
Online catalogue allows you to trawl material from the four county archive branch offices in Barrow, Carlisle, Kendal and Whitehaven.

Cumbria FHS
cumbriafhs.com

Derbyshire

Derbyshire Record Office
derbyshire.gov.uk/leisure/record_office/

Derbyshire FHS
dfhs.org.uk

Chesterfield and District FHS
cadfhs.org.uk

Devon

Devon Archives and Local Studies Service
devon.gov.uk/record_office.htm

Devon FHS
www.devonfhs.org.uk

Dorset

Dorset History Centre
dorsetforyou.com/dorsethistorycentre

Dorset FHS
dorsetfhs.org.uk

Somerset and Dorset FHS
sdfhs.org

Durham

Durham County Record Office
www.durhamrecordoffice.org.uk

Indexes to the Durham Miners' Association trade union records; 34,500 indexed images from the archive's Durham Light Infantry collection.

Durham University Library
familyrecords.dur.ac.uk

Holds important genealogical collections such as a catalogue to 150,000+ probate records (1527–1857) from the Diocese of Durham. Others include Bishops' Transcripts, Marriage Licences, Tithe Records, Estates and more.

Tyne and Wear Archives
twmuseums.org.uk/tyne-and-wear-archives.html

Northumberland and Durham FHS
ndfhs.org.uk

Cleveland, North Yorkshire and South Durham FHS
clevelandfhs.org.uk

Essex

Essex Record Office
essex.gov.uk/Libraries-Archives/Record-Office/Pages/Record-Office.aspx

Unlike many archives, ERO has its own subscription hub, Essex Ancestors, which offers access to collections via the catalogue: seax.essexcc.gov.uk.

Essex Society for FH
esfh.org.uk

East of London FHS
eolfhs.org.uk

Waltham Forest FHS
wffhs.org.uk

Gloucestershire

Gloucestershire Archives
gloucestershire.gov.uk/archives/article/107703/Archives-Homepage

Gloucestershire FHS
gfhs.org.uk

Bristol and Avon FHS
bafhs.org.uk

Forest of Dean FHT
forest-of-dean.net

Hampshire

Hampshire Archives and Local Studies
hants.gov.uk/archives
The catalogue allows you trawl more than 110,000 wills by name.

Isle of Wight Record Office
iwight.com/Residents/Libraries-Cultural-and-Heritage/Records-Office

Portsmouth History Centre and Records Office
portsmouth.gov.uk/ext/events-parks-and-whats-on/libraries/portsmouth-history-centre-and-records-office.aspx

Southampton Archives
southampton.gov.uk/archives

Hampshire Genealogical Society
hgs-online.org.uk

Isle of Wight FHS
isle-of-wight-fhs.co.uk

Herefordshire

Herefordshire Archives
www.herefordshire.gov.uk/archives

Herefordshire FHS
herefordshirefhs.org.uk

Hertfordshire

Hertfordshire Archives and Local Studies
hertsdirect.org/hals
Hertfordshire Names Online is a collection of indexes to sources such as marriage registers, wills and court registers.

Hertfordshire FHS
hertsfhs.org.uk

Letchworth and District FHG
ldfhg.org.uk

Royston and District FHS
roystonfhs.org.uk

Stevenage FHS
stevenagefhs.webspace.virginmedia.com

Huntingdonshire

Huntingdonshire Archives
www.cambridgeshire.gov.uk/info/20011/archives_archaeology_and_museums /177/archives

Covers the area of the modern Huntingdonshire District Council, plus Alwalton, Stanground, the Ortons, and Fletton, which today form part of Peterborough city.

Huntingdonshire FHS
huntsfhs.org.uk

Fenland FHS
fenlandfhs.org.uk

Kent

Kent History and Library Centre
kent.gov.uk/archives

Medway Archives
cityark.medway.gov.uk/about/medway_archives/

Very basic website, but via Medway Ancestors you can access images of original parish registers from the Archdeaconry of Rochester. The Friends of Medway Archives has also compiled a database of First World War casualties: foma-lsc.org.

Kent FHS
kfhs.org.uk

Folkestone and District FHS
folkfhs.org.uk

North West Kent FHS
nwkfhs.org.uk

Tunbridge Wells FHS
tunwells-fhs.co.uk

Lancashire

Lancashire Archives
lancashire.gov.uk/libraries-and-archives/archives-and-record-office.aspx

A search of the archives leads to a registers guide, catalogue, the North West Sound Archive, old maps of Lancashire and a police records database (1840–1925).

Lancashire Lantern
lanternimages.lancashire.gov.uk
Collections of local photographs, postcards and other images.

Manchester Archives and Local History
manchester.gov.uk/info/448/archives_and_local_history

Liverpool Libraries and Archives
liverpool.gov.uk/libraries/archives-family-history/

Lancashire FH and HS
lfhhs.org.uk

Furness FHS
furnessfhs.co.uk

Lancaster FHG
lfhg.org

Liverpool and South West Lancashire FHS
liverpool-genealogy.org.uk

Ormskirk and District FHS
odfhs.org.uk

St Helens Townships FHS
sthelenstownshipsfhs.org.uk

Wigan F and LHS
wiganworld.co.uk/familyhistory/

Leicestershire and Rutland

Record Office for Leicestershire, Leicester and Rutland
www.leics.gov.uk/recordoffice
See also Image Leicestershire at imageleicestershire.org.uk.

Leicestershire and Rutland FHS
lrfhs.org.uk

Lincolnshire

Lincolnshire Archives
www.lincolnshire.gov.uk/archives
Also try Lincs To The Past (www.lincstothepast.com) where you can search image collections, including original parish registers and a database of Lincolnshire convicts, along with sections on industry, medicine, memorials and much more.

Lincolnshire FHS
lincolnshirefhs.org.uk

Isle of Axholme FHS
axholme-fhs.org.uk

Peterborough and District FHS
peterborofhs.org.uk

London

AIM25
www.aim25.ac.uk

Barking and Dagenham, History, Heritage and Archives
www.lbbd.gov.uk/residents/leisure-libraries-and-museums/history-heritage-and-archives/

Barnet, Local Studies and Archives
www.barnet.gov.uk/info/200111/local_studies_and_archives/702/local_studies_and_archives

Bexley, Local Studies and Archive Centre
www.bexley.gov.uk/index.aspx?articleid=2563#cn2109
You can also try Bexley Borough Photos (boroughphotos.org/bexley/).

Brent Archives
brent.gov.uk/archives
There's also the Brent Archive and Museum Collection site at: brent.adlibsoft.com.

Bromley Local Studies Library and Archives
www.bromley.gov.uk/info/1062/libraries_-_local_collections/377/local_studies_library_and_archives

Camden Local Studies and Archives Centre
www.camden.gov.uk/ccm/navigation/leisure/local-history/

Croydon Records and Archives
www.croydon.gov.uk/leisure/archives

Ealing Local History Centre
www.ealing.gov.uk/info/200064/local_history/1888/local_history_centre

East of London FHS
eolfhs.org.uk

Enfield Local Studies Library and Archive
www.enfield.gov.uk/info/200048/museums_and_heritage

Greenwich Heritage Centre
www.royalgreenwich.gov.uk/info/10053/heritage_services/251/greenwich_heritage_centre

Guildhall Library
cityoflondon.gov.uk/things-to-do/visiting-the-city/archives-and-city-history/guildhall-library/Pages/default.aspx

Hackney Archives and Local History
www.hackney.gov.uk/ca-archives.htm#.VLRKvFp177V

Hammersmith and Fulham Archives
www.lbhf.gov.uk/Directory/Leisure_and_Culture/Libraries/Archives/17430_Archives_and_Local_History.asp

Haringey Archive Service
www.haringey.gov.uk/index/community_and_leisure/time_out_in_haringey/visiting_haringey/archives.htm

Harrow Local History Centre
www.harrow.gov.uk/info/200070/museums_and_galleries/183/harrow_local_history_centre

Havering Local Studies
arena.yourlondonlibrary.net/web/havering

Hillingdon Local Studies, Archives and Museums
www.hillingdon.gov.uk/article/8976/Local-studies-archives-and-museum-service

Hillingdon FHS
hfhs.co.uk

Hounslow Local History and Archives
www.hounslow.info/libraries/local-history-archives

Islington Local History Centre
www.islington.gov.uk/islington/history-heritage/heritage_lhc/Pages/default.aspx

Kensington and Chelsea Local Studies and Archives
www.rbkc.gov.uk/libraries/localstudiesandarchives.aspx
There's also the virtual museum at www.rbkc.gov.uk/virtualmuseum/.

Kingston Local History Room and Archives
www.kingston.gov.uk/info/200239/museum_archives_and_local_history/548/local_history_room_and_archives

Lambeth Archives
lambeth.gov.uk/places/lambeth-archives

Lewisham Local History and Archives Centre
www.lewisham.gov.uk/inmyarea/history/archives/Pages/default.aspx

London Metropolitan Archives
www.cityoflondon.gov.uk/things-to-do/visiting-the-city/archives-and-city-history/london-metropolitan-archives/Pages/default.aspx

London, Westminster and Middlesex FHS
lwmfhs.org.uk

Merton Heritage and Local Studies Centre
arena.yourlondonlibrary.net/web/merton/heritage
There's also Merton Memories Photographic Archive (photoarchive.merton.gov.uk).

Newham Archives and Local Studies Library
www.newham.gov.uk/pages/servicechild/newham-archives-and-local-studies-library.aspx

Redbridge Heritage
www2.redbridge.gov.uk/cms/leisure_and_libraries/libraries/your_local_library/ilford_central_library/information_and_heritage/heritage_resources.aspx

Richmond Local Studies Collection
www.richmond.gov.uk/local_studies_collection

Southwark Local History Library and Archive
www.southwark.gov.uk/info/200161/local_history_library

Sutton Archives and Local Studies
www.sutton.gov.uk/index.aspx?articleid=15674

Tower Hamlets Local History Library and Archives
www.towerhamlets.gov.uk/lgsl/1001-1050/1034_local_history__archives.aspx

Waltham Forest Archives and Local Studies Library
www.walthamforest.gov.uk/archives-local-studies

Wandsworth History and Heritage
www.wandsworth.gov.uk/homepage/215/local_history_and_heritage

(City of) Westminster Archives Centre
www.westminster.gov.uk/archives

Waltham Forest FHS
wffhs.org.uk

West Middlesex FHS
west-middlesex-fhs.org.uk

Woolwich and District FHS
woolwichfhs.org.uk

Norfolk

Norfolk Record Office
archives.norfolk.gov.uk
You can find the latest news, articles and interesting items from the vaults via the blog at: norfolkrecordofficeblog.org.

Norfolk FHS
norfolkfhs.org.uk

Mid-Norfolk FHS
tsites.co.uk/sites/mnfhs/

Northamptonshire

Archives, Heritage and History
northamptonshire.gov.uk/heritage

Northamptonshire FHS
northants-fhs.org

Peterborough and District FHS
peterborofhs.org.uk

Northumberland

Woodhorn Museum and Northumberland Archives
experiencewoodhorn.com
There's also the dedicated Museums and Archives Northumberland site at: manorthumberland.org.uk.

Tyne and Wear Archives
twmuseums.org.uk/tyne-and-wear-archives.html

Northumberland and Durham FHS
ndfhs.org.uk

Nottinghamshire

Nottinghamshire Archives
nottinghamshire.gov.uk/archives
Covers the county and the city of Nottingham. The site has details of a Nottinghamshire Memorials Project and parish register finding aids.

Nottinghamshire FHS
nottsfhs.org.uk

Oxfordshire

Oxfordshire History Centre
www.oxfordshire.gov.uk/cms/public-site/oxfordshire-history-centre

Oxfordshire FHS
ofhs.org.uk

Shropshire

Shropshire Archives
shropshire.gov.uk/archives/

Shropshire FHS
sfhs.org.uk

Somerset

Somerset Record Office
www1.somerset.gov.uk/archives/
The catalogue has 480,000 entries, also covering Bath and North East Somerset Record Office. Online indexes include Somerset Wills (1812–57), Bridgwater Shipping Crew Lists and prisoners in Ilchester Gaol.

Bath Archives
batharchives.co.uk
The online Bath Ancestors Database covers 1603 to 1990 and contains information taken from a wide variety of original records.

Somerset and Dorset FHS
sdfhs.org

Bristol and Avon FHS
bafhs.org.uk

Weston-super-Mare and District FHS
wsmfhs.org.uk

Staffordshire

Staffordshire and Stoke-on-Trent Archive Service
staffordshire.gov.uk / leisure / archives / homepage.aspx

The archive service has a number of spin-off sites such as the Sutherland Papers collection (www.sutherlandcollection.org.uk), Staffordshire Views (www.views. staffspast track.org.uk), the Great War Staffordshire (staffordshiregreatwar.com), and the very useful Staffordshire Name Indexes (www.staffsnameindexes.org.uk) – which has a number of county databases, from prisoners and apprentices to wills and parish clerks.

Birmingham Archives and Heritage
birmingham.gov.uk / archives

Wolverhampton City Archives
wolverhamptonart.org.uk / about-wolverhampton-archives /

Black Country History
blackcountryhistory.org

Birmingham and Midland Society for Genealogy and Heraldry
bmsgh.org

Burntwood FHG
bfhg.org.uk

Suffolk

Suffolk Record Office
www.suffolk.gov.uk / sro

Also try Suffolk Heritage Direct (suffolkheritagedirect.org.uk).

Suffolk FHS
suffolkfhs.org.uk

Alde Valley Suffolk FHG
aldevalleyfamilyhistorygroup.onesuffolk.net

Felixstowe FHS
www.itgen.co.uk / ffhs /

Surrey

Surrey History Centre
surreycc.gov.uk / recreation-heritage-and-culture / archives-and-history / surrey-history-centre

There's also: exploringsurreyspast.org.uk.

East Surrey FHS
eastsurreyfhs.org.uk

West Surrey FHS
wsfhs.org

Sussex

East Sussex Record Office, The Keep
eastsussex.gov.uk/useourarchives

West Sussex Record Office and Archives
www.westsussex.gov.uk/leisure/record_office_and_archives.aspx

Brighton Pavilion, Museums and Libraries
brightonmuseums.org.uk

Sussex FHG
sfhg.org.uk

Eastbourne and District FHS
eastbournefhs.org.uk

Hastings and Rother FHS
hrfhs.org.uk

Warwickshire

Warwickshire County Record Office
heritage.warwickshire.gov.uk/warwickshire-county-record-office/
This site has online databases of tithe apportionments, licensed victuallers (1801–28) and prisoners (1800–1900). There's also a catalogue called Warwickshire's Past Unlocked (archivesunlocked.warwickshire.gov.uk/calmview/) and image collections at: www.windowsonwarwickshire.org.uk.

Birmingham and Midland Society for Genealogy and Heraldry
bmsgh.org

Coventry FHS
covfhs.org.uk

Nuneaton and North Warwickshire FHS
nnwfhs.org.uk

Rugby FHG
rugbyfhg.co.uk

Wiltshire

Wiltshire and Swindon History Centre
wshc.eu

The centre houses the Salisbury Diocesan Probate collection of 105,000 wills (1540–1858). Thanks to the Wiltshire Wills Project you can search the collection by name, place, occupation and date at: history.wiltshire.gov.uk/heritage/, and for a fee you can view original images.

Wiltshire FHS
wiltshirefhs.co.uk

Worcestershire

Worcestershire Archive and Archaeology Service
thehiveworcester.org

The site has databases covering photographs, maps and schools, plus a host of online indexes – from absent voters to Worcester Royal Grammar School Admission Registers (1850–1913). There's also a blog at explorethepast.co.uk.

Birmingham and Midland Society for Genealogy and Heraldry
bmsgh.org

Malvern FHS
mfhs.org.uk

Yorkshire

East Riding of Yorkshire Archives, Family and Local History
www2.eastriding.gov.uk/leisure/archives-family-and-local-history/

North Yorkshire Record Office
northyorks.gov.uk/article/23584

You can also browse images and maps via the online shop at: archiveshop. northyorks.gov.uk.

West Yorkshire Archives Service
archives.wyjs.org.uk

Home to the important West Riding Registry of Deeds, which was established in 1704 and operated until 1970. The service runs offices in Wakefield, Bradford, Calderdale (Halifax), Kirklees (Huddersfield) and Leeds.

Borthwick Institute for Archives, University of York
york.ac.uk/borthwick/

The institute holds important collections, some of which are already online. There's the Cause Papers database (hrionline.ac.uk/causepapers/), through which you can explore church court records between 1300 and 1858, and the institute recently won a grant to digitize twenty-one archbishops' registers (1225–1646). There's also the blog at: borthwickinstitute.blogspot.co.uk.

Local and Family History Library, Leeds
www.leeds.gov.uk/leisure/Pages/Local-and-family-history-service.aspx
See also the dated but functioning photographic library at www.leodis.net.

Sheffield Archives and Local Studies
www.sheffield.gov.uk/libraries/archives-and-local-studies.html
Also try the image library at: picturesheffield.com.

Sheffield Indexers
sheffieldindexers.com
Special mention for this wonderful collective, which offers vast quantities of transcribed and indexed sources relating to the area.

York Libraries and Archives
exploreyork.org.uk

Hull History Centre
hullhistorycentre.org.uk
This centre has lots of useful guides to sources, such as important maritime material which includes 25,000 crew lists.

Teesside Archives
middlesbrough.gov.uk/teessidearchives

University of Huddersfield Heritage Quay
heritagequay.org

Barnsley FHS
barnsleyfhs.co.uk

Bradford FHS
bradfordfhs.org.uk

Calderdale FHS
cfhsweb.com

City of York and District FHS
yorkfamilyhistory.org.uk

Cleveland, North Yorkshire and South Durham FHS
clevelandfhs.org.uk

Doncaster and District FHS
doncasterfhs.co.uk

East Yorkshire FHS
eyfhs.org.uk

Harrogate and District FHS
hadfhs.co.uk

Huddersfield and District FHS
hdfhs.org.uk

Keighley and District FHS
kdfhs.org.uk

Pontefract and District FHS
pontefractfhs.org.uk

Ripon Historical Society and FHG
riponhistoricalsociety.org.uk

Rotherham FHS
rotherhamfhs.co.uk

Ryedale FHG
ryedalefamilyhistory.org

Selby and District FHG
selbydistrictfamilyhistory.btck.co.uk

Sheffield and District FHS
sheffieldfhs.org.uk

Wakefield and District FHS
wdfhs.co.uk

Wharfedale FHG
wharfedalefhg.org.uk

REGIONAL: WALES

Anglesey

Anglesey Records and Archives
www.anglesey.gov.uk/leisure/records-and-archives/

Gwynedd FHS
gwyneddfhs.org

Breconshire (Brecknockshire)

Powys Archives
archives.powys.gov.uk

Powys FHS
powysfhs.org.uk

Caernarvonshire

Gwynedd Archives Service
gwynedd.gov.uk/archives
Runs the Caernarvon and Meirionnydd record offices.

Gwynedd FHS
gwyneddfhs.org

Cardiganshire (Ceredigion)

Ceredigion Archives
archifdy-ceredigion.org.uk

Cardiganshire FHS
cgnfhs.org.uk

Dyfed FHS
dyfedfhs.org.uk

Carmarthenshire (Sir Caerfyrddin)

Carmarthenshire Archives Service
www.carmarthenshire.gov.uk/english/leisure/archives/pages/archivesrecords.
aspx

Dyfed FHS
dyfedfhs.org.uk

Denbighshire

Denbighshire Archives
www.denbighshire.gov.uk/en/resident/libraries-and-archives/denbighshire-
archives/denbighshire-archives.aspx

Clwyd FHS
clwydfhs.org.uk

Flintshire

Flintshire Record Office
www.flintshire.gov.uk/en/LeisureAndTourism/Records-and-Archives/Home.aspx

There is a catalogue and a large number of useful indexes available. Go to Records and Archives > Databases > Subjects.

Clwyd FHS
clwydfhs.org.uk

Glamorgan

Glamorgan Archives
glamarchives.gov.uk

Visit the blog at: glamarchives.wordpress.com.

West Glamorgan Archive Service
swansea.gov.uk/westglamorganarchives

Glamorgan FHS
glamfhs.org.uk

Merionethshire

Gwynedd Archives Service
gwynedd.gov.uk/archives

Gwynedd FHS
gwyneddfhs.org

Monmouthshire

Gwent Archives
gwentarchives.gov.uk

Opened its new site in Ebbw Vale in 2011. Gwent comprises most of Monmouthshire and a small part of Breconshire – the rest of Monmouthshire is part of modern Glamorgan.

Gwent FHS
gwentfhs.info

Montgomeryshire

Powys Archives
archives.powys.gov.uk

Remember to check Herefordshire and Shropshire archives too.

Montgomeryshire Genealogical Society
montgomeryshiregs.org.uk

Powys FHS
powysfhs.org.uk

Pembrokeshire

Pembrokeshire Archives
www.pembrokeshire.gov.uk/content.asp?nav=107,1447
Recently opened in its new home in Haverfordwest.

Dyfed FHS
dyfedfhs.org.uk

Radnorshire

Powys Archives
archives.powys.gov.uk
Again, Herefordshire and Shropshire archives may also hold relevant material.

Powys FHS
powysfhs.org.uk

REGIONAL: SCOTLAND

Aberdeenshire

Aberdeen City and Aberdeenshire Archives
aberdeencity.gov.uk/archives
Lots of useful online tools including indexes to baptism registers, militia records, tax rolls, plus images on HistoryPin. You could also try Aberdeen University's Burgh Records Database Project (abdn.ac.uk/aberdeen-burgh-records-database/). Aberdeen burial records are available via DeceasedOnline.

Aberdeen and North East Scotland FHS
anesfhs.org.uk

Angus

Angus Archives
www.angus.gov.uk/history/archives/

Dundee City Archives
dundeecity.gov.uk/archive

Tay Valley FHS
tayvalleyfhs.org.uk

Aberdeen and North East Scotland FHS
anesfhs.org.uk

Friends of Dundee City Archives
fdca.org.uk

Argyll

Argyll and Bute Archives
argyll-bute.gov.uk/community-life-and-leisure/archives

Glasgow and West of Scotland FHS
gwsfhs.org.uk

Highland FHS
highlandfamilyhistorysociety.org

Lochaber and North Argyll Family History Group
lochaberandnorthargyllfamilyhistorygroup.org.uk

Ayrshire

Ayrshire Archives Online
ayrshirearchives.org.uk
Runs archive centres in Ayr, Saltcoats and Kilmarnock.

Alloway and Southern Ayrshire FHS
asafhs.co.uk

Glasgow and West of Scotland FHS
gwsfhs.org.uk

Troon and Ayrshire FHS
troonayrshirefhs.org.uk

Banffshire

Aberdeen City and Aberdeenshire Archives
aberdeencity.gov.uk/archives

Aberdeen and North East Scotland FHS
anesfhs.org.uk

Berwickshire

Scottish Borders Archive and Local History Centre
www.scotborders.gov.uk/info/476/local_history_heritage_and_museums/32/
heritage_hub
You could also try Eyemouth Museum (eyemouthmuseum.org).

Borders FHS
bordersfhs.org.uk

Buteshire

Argyll and Bute Archives
argyll-bute.gov.uk/community-life-and-leisure/archives
You could also try Bute Museum (www.butemuseum.org.uk/archives/).

Glasgow and West of Scotland FHS
gwsfhs.org.uk

Caithness

Highland Archives Service
highlandarchives.org.uk/caithness.asp
Runs the Skye and Lochalsh, Caithness, Lochaber and Highland Archive Centres.

Caithness FHS
caithnessfhs.org.uk

Highland FHS
highlandfamilyhistorysociety.org

Clackmannanshire

Clackmannanshire Archives
clacksweb.org.uk/culture/archives/

Central Scotland FHS
csfhs.org.uk

Dumfriesshire

Dumfries and Galloway Libraries and Archives
www.dumgal.gov.uk/lia
You can explore lots of useful indexes produced by the Friends of the Archives of Dumfries and Galloway at: info.dumgal.gov.uk/HistoricalIndexes/.

Dumfries and Galloway FHS
dgfhs.org.uk

Dunbartonshire

East Dunbartonshire Archives
www.edlc.co.uk/heritage/archives.aspx

West Dunbartonshire Council Archives
west-dunbarton.gov.uk/libraries/archives-family-history/archives-collections/
Runs the Clydebank and Dumbarton heritage centres.

Glasgow and West of Scotland FHS
gwsfhs.org.uk

East Lothian

John Gray Centre – Library, Museum and Archive
www.johngraycentre.org

Lothians FHS
lothiansfhs.org

Edinburgh

Edinburgh City Archives
www.edinburgh.gov.uk/info/20032/access_to_information/600/edinburgh_city
_archives

There's also the blog at lothianlives.org.uk.

Fife

Fife Archive Centre
fifedirect.org.uk/archives

The centre has a number of online finding aids, including indexes to schools, a poorhouse, evacuees, miners and police.

Fife FHS
fifefhs.org

Tay Valley FHS
tayvalleyfhs.org.uk

Glasgow

Glasgow Family History, Mitchell Library
glasgowfamilyhistory.org.uk

Family history resources at the Mitchell Library are made up of records from the Glasgow City Archives, the registrars' service, the library's Special Collections and the NHS Greater Glasgow and Clyde Archives. The site details burial records, BMD data, census material and there's a complete A–Z of research guides.

Inverness-shire

Highland Archives Service
highlandarchives.org.uk/harc.asp
Runs the Highland Archive Centre in Inverness.

Highland FHS
highlandfamilyhistorysociety.org

Kincardineshire

Aberdeen City and Aberdeenshire Archives
aberdeencity.gov.uk/archives

Aberdeen and North East Scotland FHS
anesfhs.org.uk

Kinross-shire

Perth and Kinross Archives
www.pkc.gov.uk/archives

Tay Valley FHS
tayvalleyfhs.org.uk

Kirkcudbrightshire

Dumfries and Galloway Libraries and Archives
www.dumgal.gov.uk/lia

Dumfries and Galloway FHS
dgfhs.org.uk

Lanarkshire

North Lanarkshire Archives
www.northlanarkshire.gov.uk/archives
Also runs local and family studies centres in Airdrie and Motherwell, as well as Bellshill Family History Centre.

South Lanarkshire Archives
www.southlanarkshire.gov.uk/info/200165/local_and_family_history/588/archives_and_records

Lanarkshire FHS
lanarkshirefhs.org.uk

Midlothian

Midlothian Local Studies Centre, Loanhead
www.midlothian.gov.uk/info/476/family_history_archives_and_local_history

Edinburgh City Archives
www.edinburgh.gov.uk/info/20032/access_to_information/600/edinburgh_city_
archives

There's also the blog at lothianlives.org.uk.

Moray

Moray Council Local Heritage Centre
www.moray.gov.uk/moray_standard/page_1537.html

Moray and Nairn FHS
morayandnairnfhs.co.uk

Moray Burial Ground Research Group
mbgrg.org

Nairnshire

Highland Archive Centre
highlandarchives.org.uk/harc.asp
Includes official records of Nairnshire.

Highland FHS
highlandfamilyhistorysociety.org

Orkney

Orkney Library and Archive
www.orkneylibrary.org.uk

Orkney FHS
orkneyfhs.co.uk

Peeblesshire

Scottish Borders Archive and Local History Centre
www.scotborders.gov.uk/info/476/local_history_heritage_and_museums/32/
heritage_hub

Borders FHS
bordersfhs.org.uk

Perthshire

Perth and Kinross Archive
www.pkc.gov.uk/archives

University of Dundee Archives
dundee.ac.uk/archives/

Dundee City Archive and Record Centre
www.dundeecity.gov.uk/archive/

Tay Valley FHS
tayvalleyfhs.org.uk

Central Scotland FHS
csfhs.org.uk

Renfrewshire

East Renfrewshire Archives
eastrenfrewshire.gov.uk/archives
There's also East Renfrewshire Council's local history and heritage website: www.portaltothepast.co.uk

Renfrewshire Heritage Services, Paisley Central Library
www.renfrewshire.gov.uk/webcontent/home/Services/Libraries/Heritage_Services/

Renfrewshire FHS
renfrewshirefhs.co.uk

Glasgow and West of Scotland FHS
gwsfhs.org.uk

Ross and Cromarty

Highland Archives Service
highlandarchives.org.uk/genealogy.asp
The service looks after records relating to Inverness, Nairn, Ross and Cromarty, and Sutherland.

Glasgow and West of Scotland FHS
gwsfhs.org.uk

Highland FHS
highlandfamilyhistorysociety.org

Roxburghshire

Scottish Borders Archives, Heritage Hub, Hawick
www.heartofhawick.co.uk/info/1/about_us/12/heritage_hub

Borders FHS
bordersfhs.org.uk

Selkirkshire

Scottish Borders Archives, Heritage Hub, Hawick
www.heartofhawick.co.uk/info/1/about_us/12/heritage_hub

Borders FHS
bordersfhs.org.uk

Shetland

Shetland Museum and Archives
shetland-museum.org.uk
Now has an archive catalogue at: www.calmview.eu/ShetlandArchive/Calm
View/. There's also a really good image library at: photos.shetland-museum.
org.uk.

Shetland FHS
shetland-fhs.org.uk

Stirlingshire

Stirling Archives
stirling.gov.uk/archives

Falkirk Archives
www.falkirkcommunitytrust.org/heritage/archives/
There's also the Falkirk Museums and Archives collections site at collections.
falkirk.gov.uk.

Central Scotland FHS
csfhs.org.uk

Sutherland

Highland Archives Service
highlandarchives.org.uk/genealogy.asp
The service looks after records relating to Inverness, Nairn, Ross and Cromarty,
and Sutherland.

Highland FHS
highlandfamilyhistorysociety.org

West Lothian

West Lothian Council Archives and Records Centre
www.westlothian.gov.uk/article/2052/Archives

Lothians FHS
lothiansfhs.org

Wigtownshire

Dumfries and Galloway Libraries and Archives
www.dumgal.gov.uk/lia

Dumfries and Galloway FHS
dgfhs.org.uk

REGIONAL: NORTHERN IRELAND

Antrim, Armagh, Down, Fermanagh, Londonderry, Tyrone

Public Record Office of Northern Ireland
www.proni.gov.uk
Online Records include Will Calendars, Valuation Revision Books, Street Directories, the Ulster Covenant, Freeholders Records and Londonderry Corporation Records. Additionally, there's material on CAIN (Conflict Archive on the INternet) and material on YouTube/Flickr.

Derry Genealogy Centre
derrycity.gov.uk/Genealogy/Derry-Genealogy
Also via derry.rootsireland.ie you can access the mass database to pre-1922 civil birth and marriage registers, early BMD registers of 85 churches (26 Roman Catholic Church, 24 Church of Ireland and 35 Presbyterian), and gravestone inscriptions from 117 graveyards, plus pre-1910 registers of Derry City Cemetery. There's also the index to 1901 census returns and to Griffith's Valuation of 1858/1859.

Belfast City Council Burials
www.belfastcity.gov.uk/burialrecords/index.asp
Look up 360,000 burial records from the Belfast City (from 1869 onwards), Roselawn (from 1954 onwards) and Dundonald (from 1905 onwards) Cemeteries.

Linen Hall Library
linenhall.com
The main library in Belfast.

National Archives of Ireland
nationalarchives.ie

North of Ireland FHS
nifhs.org

Irish Genealogy Research Society
irishancestors.ie

REGIONAL: THE ISLE OF MAN

iMuseum
www.imuseum.im

'Home of Manx Memories.' For a charge you can explore 400,000 pages of digitized newspapers. There's also a general family history search page, allowing you to trawl through a number of key genealogical sources.

Isle of Man Library and Archives
manxnationalheritage.im

Isle of Man FHS
iomfhs.im

REGIONAL: THE CHANNEL ISLANDS

Jersey, Guernsey, Alderney, Sark, Herm

Genuki, The Channel Islands
chi.genuki.weald.org.uk

Jersey Archive
jerseyheritage.org/places-to-visit/jersey-archive

Search church and parish registers via search.jerseyheritage.org.

Island Archives – Guernsey
www.gov.gg/islandarchives

Alderney Society
alderneysociety.org/museum_collections.php

Priaulx Library
priaulxlibrary.co.uk

The Channel Islands FHS
jerseyfamilyhistory.org

La Société Guernesiaise
societe.org.gg/sections/familyhistory.php

OTHER SOCIETIES

Overseas and Special Interest

Anglo-German FHS
agfhs.org

Anglo-Italian FHS
anglo-italianfhs.org.uk

Association of Genealogists and Researchers in Archives
agra.org.uk

Australasian Federation of Family History Organisations
affho.org

British Association for Local History
balh.co.uk

Catholic FHS
www.catholic-history.org.uk/cfhs

Families in British India Society
fibis.org

Federation of Family History Societies
ffhs.org.uk

Federation of Genealogical Societies, USA
fgs.org

Guild of One-Name Studies
one-name.org

Heraldry Society
theheraldrysociety.com

Institute of Heraldic and Genealogical Studies
ihgs.ac.uk

Jewish Genealogical Society of Great Britain
jgsgb.org.uk

New Zealand Society of Genealogists
genealogy.org.nz

Quaker FHS
qfhs.co.uk

Romany and Traveller FHS
rtfhs.org.uk

Society of Australian Genealogists
sag.org.au

5.2 Blogs and Forums

Forums and blogs can be a platform for sharing your knowledge, posing questions, or just finding out more about the wider digital community. The collaborative nature of forums in particular means that even if you don't feel like posing a question, you may well find useful correspondence between researchers who have found themselves in similar situations.

Rootschat
rootschat.com

The 'UK's largest free family history forum' is indeed thriving, with lots of specialist sections and threads. Scroll down the homepage and there are sections for beginners; dating and restoring old photos; subjects relating to the armed forces; and lots more. The archived Reference Library has threads going back to 2003.

Great War Forum
1914-1918.invisionzone.com/forums/

This is a specialist First World War forum created by Chris Baker, the man behind the Long, Long, Trail website (1914-1918.net). You can post pictures, perhaps showing your ancestor in uniform, or showing some insignia or cap badge, and put out information requests.

Birmingham History Forum
birminghamhistory.co.uk/forum/

An example of a bustling regional history hub. Such forums can be really useful for finding out more about individual institutions, or little-known local sources. Users are quick to post useful links too.

Who Do You Think You Are? Magazine Forum

whodoyouthinkyouaremagazine.com/forum/

Official magazine forum which also has a spin-off app. At time of writing the most popular sections were Research help and Photo identification.

Geneabloggers

geneabloggers.com

Seeks to coalesce the genealogical blogging community. You can also follow @geneabloggers on Twitter.

Cyndi's List blog

cyndislist.blogspot.co.uk

This is Cyndi's own blog, and you can also find the site's own list of genealogical blogs at: cyndislist.com/blogs.htm.

Victorian Wars Forum

victorianwars.com

British military campaigns from 1837 to 1902.

The British GENES Blog (Genealogy News and Events)

britishgenes.blogspot.com

DNA Forums

forums.familytreedna.com/

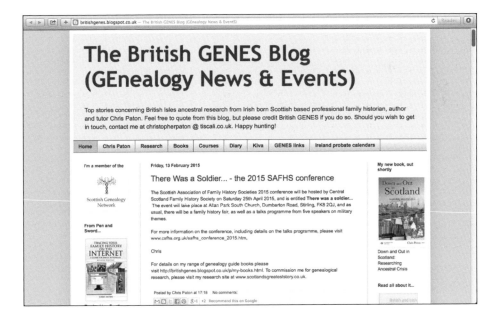

Family History Research Wiki
familysearch.org/learn/wiki/en/Main_Page

GenForum, Genealogy.com
genforum.genealogy.com

LostCousins Genealogy Forums
forums.lc/genealogy/index.php

British Genealogy and Family History Forums
british-genealogy.com

Family History UK Genealogy Forums
forum.familyhistory.uk.com

Historum
historum.com

British Medal Forum
britishmedalforum.com

AngloBoerWar.com Forum
angloboerwar.com/forum

Dick Eastman's Genealogy Newsletter
blog.eogn.com

Anglo-Celtic-Connections
anglo-celtic-connections.blogspot.com

Wandering Genealogist
wanderinggenealogist.wordpress.com/

Genetic Genealogist
thegeneticgenealogist.com

Tracing the Tribe
tracingthetribe.blogspot.com

Grow Your Own Family Tree
growyourownfamilytree.wordpress.com

Genealogy Guys
genealogyguys.com

Lineagekeeper's Genealogy Blog
leedrew.com

Olive Tree Genealogy blog
olivetreegenealogy.blogspot.com

Genealogy and History News
gouldgenealogy.com

Footnote Maven
footnotemaven.com

The Victorianist
thevictorianist.blogspot.co.uk

The 23andMe Blog
blog.23andme.com

Findmypast blog
blog.findmypast.co.uk

Ancestry.co.uk Blog
blogs.ancestry.com/uk/

GenealogyBlog
genealogyblog.com

See also: 5.7 Sharing Research, 5.8 Social Networking, 5.9 Software and Apps

5.3 House History

Researching the history of your house, or any building in which your ancestor lived, draws on many sources that are familiar to genealogists, such as census returns, maps and plans, rate books and taxation records, probate material and deeds.

BuildingHistory
buildinghistory.org

Jean Manco's website has a functional, basic design, but is packed with advice, information and useful links, and there's no annoying advertising. You could start with the Basics page, a short section on evaluating sources, or go straight to Building Types to find relevant guidance.

Manorial Documents Register
discovery.nationalarchives.gov.uk

Formerly located on a dedicated page and now integrated into TNA's Discovery, the Manorial Documents Register records the location of manorial court documents in England and Wales, which can provide information about land and property, and include court rolls, surveys, maps, terriers and documents relating to boundaries.

Images of England

www.imagesofengland.org.uk

English Heritage photo survey of listed buildings. You can find out more about English Heritage's archives and collections via english-heritage.org.uk/professional/ archives-and-collections/nmr/archives/photographs/. Finally there's this page with advice about starting your own house history: english-heritage.org.uk/your-home/your-homes-history/.

Vision of Britain

visionofbritain.org.uk

Type in an address or a postcode and an historic map of the area appears, with the option to view other examples covering the same area back to 1805. You can magnify to focus on individual buildings, and it enables you to quickly gain an idea of the physical surroundings through time.

ScotlandsPlaces

scotlandsplaces.gov.uk

Tailored towards researching Scotland's physical heritage, the site allows users to search archival collections by geographical location. From the homepage you can either type in a place/coordinate, or use the site's own maps to refine your search.

National Library of Scotland

maps.nls.uk

The National Library of Scotland's site provides high-resolution images of over 91,000 maps of Scotland from between 1580 to 1919. These include the important Roy Military Survey of Scotland (1747–55): maps.nls.uk/roy/.

Findmypast

findmypast.co.uk

This is not the only potential source for buildings research on Findmypast, but, since taking over Origins, the site has incorporated all the information formerly available through specialist probate site the National Wills Index.

Hearth Tax Online

hearthtax.org.uk

Provides analysis of the hearth tax, which was introduced in 1662, giving you insight into a household's status.

Royal Commission on the Ancient and Historical Monuments of Wales

www.rcahmw.gov.uk

Home to photographs, maps and more relating to the built heritage of Wales. There's also the catalogue: coflein.gov.uk.

British History Online

british-history.ac.uk

This site hosts huge amounts of material relating to land and property – not least the Victoria County Histories.

HistoryPin
historypin.com

Search for photographs of streets or buildings in the past, or upload photos from your own collection.

Hidden House History
hiddenhousehistory.co.uk

Television series spin-off.

Trace My House
tracemyhouse.com

Archives for House History, Archives Wales
archiveswales.org.uk/using-archives/archives-for-house-history/

House History Guide, Devon Heritage Centre
devon.gov.uk/house_history

See also: 1.3 The Census, 2.2 Probate and Wills, 2.3 Taxation, 2.10 Directories, 2.21 Photographs and Films, 2.23 Maps, 2.24 Estate Records, 2.25 Seventeeth- and Eighteenth-Century Sources

5.4 Medieval Ancestors

Given the difficult-to-read handwriting, abbreviated Latin, mysterious terminology, archaic and inconsistent spellings, and the fact that most genealogically useful sources relate to the landed classes, you'll soon discover why so few can claim any provable family connection to the period.

MedievalGenealogy
medievalgenealogy.org.uk

Medieval genealogy relies on a set of sources that may be unfamiliar – manorial records, government enrolments, taxation returns, heraldic visitations and court material. Chris Phillips's website not only tells you where to find documents, but also why they were created – vital for understanding and interpreting the material.

The Henry III Fine Rolls Project
frh3.org.uk

This 'window into English history' allows you to search a translated version of the 'fine rolls' – records of money offered to Henry III for various concessions and favours. It includes indexes, a search facility, digital images of the original rolls, and a running commentary from various experts.

British History Online
british-history.ac.uk

Hosts all sorts of medieval sources, and the quickest way to find them is via the Period drop-down menu. Choose eleventh and twelfth centuries to view the likes of Higher Clergy, Charters and Documents, and Monastic and Cathedral Records.

Medieval Sources Guide, The National Archives

nationalarchives.gov.uk / records / research-guides / medieval-sources-for-family-history.htm

This research guide includes a concise introduction to the major sources for medieval genealogists. You'll also find links to the Beginners' Latin and Palaeography sections of the website, plus the Domesday Book online.

People of Medieval Scotland

www.poms.ac.uk

The result of two major academic studies, this website features a consolidated database of around 21,000 individuals recorded in documents written between 1093 and 1314.

The Medieval Soldier

medievalsoldier.org

Searchable database of 220,000 soldiers compiled from muster rolls and records of protections held at TNA, plus records drawn from French repositories.

Prosopography of Anglo-Saxon England

pase.ac.uk

An attempt to record the names of all inhabitants of England from the late sixth century to the end of the eleventh century, which draws on all kinds of sources.

Domesday Book Online

domesdaybook.co.uk

Includes an alphabetized list of almost 200 of the most well-known landholders mentioned in the Domesday Book.

Medieval English Towns

users.trytel.com/~tristan/towns/towns.html

Learn about English towns during the Middle Ages.

The Foundation for Medieval Genealogy

fmg.ac

The Harleian Society

harleian.org.uk

Heraldry Society

theheraldrysociety.com

Medieval Resources Online

www.leeds.ac.uk/ims/med_online/medresource.html

Early-Modern Palaeography

paleo.anglo-norman.org/empfram.html

See also: 2.1 Probate and Wills, 2.3 Taxation, 2.6 Court Records, 2.24 Estate Records, 5.5 Heraldry, 5.6 Nobility and Gentry

5.5 Heraldry

Crests, coats of arms and other heraldic devices in your family archive won't necessarily indicate the right to bear arms. All armorial bearings are specific to a particular family or pedigree, rather than everyone who shares the surname. In England and Wales pedigrees are officially recorded in the College of Arms, whose records are vital if you're researching an entitled line.

College of Arms

college-of-arms.gov.uk

The College of Arms is the best place to familiarize yourself with the heritage, history and peculiarities of heraldry. Via Resources there's an FAQ section and the Roll of the Peerage, from Services you can learn how to prove a right to arms, while the About Us section has details of records and collections held here.

Institute of Heraldic and Genealogical Studies

ihgs.ac.uk

Via Library and Collections you can explore the sources available here – such as the comprehensive Armorial Index of over 100,000 cards. You can read about the

Andrews Index (newspaper announcements, 1790–1976) which has also been made available on Ancestry (search.ancestry.co.uk/search/db.aspx?dbid=1897).

The Court of the Lord Lyon
lyon-court.com

The heraldic authority for Scotland, which deals with Scottish heraldry and coats of arms. The Court of the Lord Lyon maintains the Scottish Public Registers of Arms and Genealogies. The site also has information about often misunderstood conventions of clans, crests and tartans.

Burke's Peerage
burkespeerage.com

The definitive guide to the pedigrees and heraldry of the landed gentry. You can search for free, but to access the data there are a number of subscription options – from full annual access (£80) to 48-hour passes (£8.95).

Heraldry on the Internet
www.digiserve.com/heraldry/

This site is no longer updated but it still links through to useful online material such as Pimbley's Dictionary of Heraldry (www.digiserve.com/heraldry/pimbley.htm).

Medieval Genealogy
medievalgenealogy.org.uk

Provides a practical introduction to medieval genealogy, including sections on all kinds of sources, such as heralds' visitations.

Office of the Chief Herald
www.nli.ie/en/heraldry-introduction.aspx

This National Library of Ireland website details the responsibilities and services of the Chief Herald of Ireland.

HeraldsNet
heraldsnet.org/saitou/parker/index.htm

Illustrated online glossary to heraldry, based on a book first published in 1894 (and not modified since 2004).

The Right to Arms, Society of Genealogists
sog.org.uk/learn/education-sub-page-for-testing-navigation/hints-tips-seven-the-right-to-arms

SoG Hints and Tips section on the Right to Arms. The SoG Library also has an extensive heraldry section.

Coats of Arms and Family Crests
coats-of-arms.blogspot.co.uk

View and download lots of coats of arms/family crests.

The Governor General of Canada
gg.ca
The Canadian heraldic authority.

Heraldry Online
heraldry-online.org.uk

The Heraldry Society
theheraldrysociety.com

The Heraldry Society of Scotland
heraldry-scotland.co.uk

Harleian Society
harleian.org.uk

Society of Antiquaries of London
sal.org.uk/library/

See also: 2.24 Estate Records, 5.4 Medieval Ancestors, 5.6 Nobility and Gentry

5.6 Nobility and Gentry

As a general rule of thumb, the richer your ancestors were, the more extensive the potential paper trail. For example, plenty of people left behind wills, but the will of a wealthy person is more likely to contain details of estates, assets, family relationships and often an exhaustive inventory of personal possessions.

British History Online
british-history.ac.uk

Explore local history material through Victoria County History volumes, which give lots of information about landed families. Plus the site has name-rich sources that are useful for researching the elite classes: 'Calendars of State Papers, for example, include information about individual appointments, titles, inheritance, and marriages, while the Catalogue of Ancient Deeds and Feet of Fines provide information about relationships within and between families.'

Burke's Peerage
burkespeerage.com

Established by John Burke in 1826, this is the online home of the 'definitive guide to the genealogy and heraldry of the Peerage, Baronetage, Knightage and Landed Gentry of the United Kingdom'. While much of the material is only accessible by subscription, there are free sections which give you an idea of the kind of material on offer here, including detailed pedigrees of prominent royal families of Europe.

Genuki
genuki.org.uk

Navigate to the list of counties, click the county and on the list of sub-categories there should be 'Nobility', which leads on to descriptions of important families and key landed estates.

Medieval Genealogy, Links
medievalgenealogy.org.uk/links/links.shtml

The links section will direct you to all kinds of sources and databases updated by researchers with an interest in pedigrees of the upper classes.

Landed Gentry of Berkshire
berkshirehistory.com/gentry/database/index.htm

A good example of a regional study, this is a genealogical database of noble, manorial, landed and heraldic families associated with Berkshire.

British Nobility, Wikipedia
en.wikipedia.org/wiki/British_nobility

Useful page that gives a rundown of the structure of British nobility. Meanwhile, for a more general description of gentry go to: en.wikipedia.org/wiki/Gentry.

Society of Genealogists
sog.org.uk

It's certainly worth exploring the SoG catalogue, as the library houses all kinds of books and sources relating to nobility, gentry and the landed classes.

Archive
archive.org

Insomniacs should trawl archive.org for stuffy Victorian and Edwardian narratives of the landed classes. Many have been digitized.

The Peerage
thepeerage.com

Genealogical survey of the peerage of Britain and royal families of Europe.

Irish Nobility and Landed Gentry
irishnobility.blogspot.co.uk

A database of free e-books relating to Irish genealogy.

See also: 2.2 Probate and Wills, 2.3 Taxation, 2.24 Estate Records, 2.25 Seventeenth- and Eighteenth-Century Sources, 5.3 House History, 5.4 Medieval Ancestors, 5.5 Heraldry

5.7 Sharing Research

Sharing your research and social networking are closely associated subjects, and some of the leading social networks are covered in the next chapter. Here you will find sites specifically designed to share your family history with friends, family and other researchers.

Lives of the First World War
livesofthefirstworldwar.org

Share your stories of First World War ancestors through this collaboration between D.C. Thomson Family History and IWM. The end result is to be a permanent digital memorial to the 8 million men and women from across Britain and the Commonwealth who served in uniform or worked on the home front.

Pinterest
uk.pinterest.com

More genealogists than you might think use Pinterest. This link takes you to the official Pinterest home of Cyndi's List: pinterest.com/cyndislist/. Another example is GeneaBloggers (interest.com/geneabloggers/), a community of 3,000 bloggers which had 155,000+ Pinterest followers at the time of writing.

Who Do You Think You Are? Story
whodoyouthinkyouarestory.com

Launched in the summer of 2014. Here you can create and share your own personalized *WDYTYA?* experience. Simply tap in some data about your pedigree and the site produces an easily shareable *WDYTYA?*-style video.

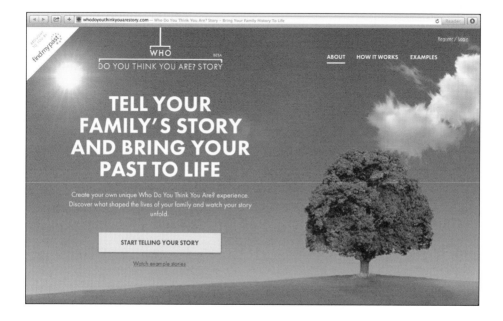

TheGenealogist

thegenealogist.co.uk

The team behind online family tree builder TreeView, which has recently been given a makeover for tablet and mobile users.

GENi

geni.com

Powerful online tree from the makers of MyHeritage. At the time of writing it claimed to connect 82 million people.

10 People Genealogists Follow on Twitter

geneabloggers.com/ten-people-genealogists-follow-twitter/

The list is: @megansmolenyak, @footnotemaven, @dickeastman, @rjseaver, @LorineMS, @marktucker, @illyadaddezio, @moultriecreek, @kidmiff and @tracingthetribe.

MyHeritage

MyHeritage.com

The leading genealogy social network, designed to help you compile and share your family history.

Twitter

twitter.com

Great place to follow your interests and share/post your own genealogical findings.

Seven Tips for Mapping Out your Ancestors on Pinterest

nelsonrainsgenealogy.blogspot.co.uk/2014/01/7-tips-for-mapping-out-your-family-on.html

Blog entry which details ways to use Pinterest (uk.pinterest.com) for genealogy.

Heir Hunter

hha-bmd.com

Upload and share certificates, wills, photos and other documents with fellow researchers.

Rodovid

en.rodovid.org

Wiki-like family tree portal, where you can access, edit and create family trees.

OurStory

ourstory.com

Share stories, photos and videos either publicly or with family and friends.

FamilyRelatives

familyrelatives.com

General commercial site, but with lots of networking features.

WhatWasThere

whatwasthere.com

Ties historical photos to Google Maps.

uencounter

uencounter.me

Another virtual pin map.

Family Crossings

familycrossings.com

Build your own family website.

Findmypast

findmypast.co.uk

GenesReunited

genesreunited.co.uk

WikiTree

wikitree.com

FamilyMe

family.me

SharedTree

sharedtree.com

StoryVault

storyvault.com

ShareHistory

sharehistory.org

Ages-Online

ages-online.com

See also: 5.2 Blogs and Forums, 5.8 Social Networking, 5.9 Software and Apps

5.8 Social Networking

Finding those with shared research interests has been the primary drive behind online genealogy since the mailing lists and newsgroups of the 1990s. And today, genealogists have taken to social networking platforms with gusto. However, it's also a subject that defies rigid definition. Commercial sites have tools that fit into the broad category of social networking. And sites that define the term, such as Facebook, have tools and third-party apps designed for family historians.

Facebook.com
facebook.com

This author isn't on Facebook. However, lots of people are. You can connect with extended family, join a group, share trees and photos and, in addition, build personalized pages telling your story; there are tailor-made tree-building apps (such as Family Tree [livefamily.com] or TheGenealogist's TreeView). You can also allow the likes of Ancestry to find Facebook profiles from people in your tree.

Twitter
twitter.com

This author is on Twitter, where at the time of writing he had a stratospheric 102 followers. But the point of Twitter is to 'follow your interests', and as such there's no quicker, easier, or more pleasurable way to connect with genealogical movers and shakers, and related heritage services such as museums and archives. I admit the following statement doesn't stand up to close scrutiny but, for me, Facebook looks backwards, Twitter looks forwards.

MyHeritage
myheritage.com

The leading genealogical social network, which allows members to create their own family websites, share pictures and videos, search for ancestors and more. The RecordMatching and SmartMatching tools are designed to connect researchers, plus it has now teamed up with DNA firm 23andMe.com to allow users with matching DNA to explore family tree connections.

HistoryPin
historypin.org

This addictive website is primarily a crowdsourcing hub, but projects are tailored to spread through social networks, and it's set up so you can connect Twitter/Facebook/Google accounts with your HistoryPin Profile. Remember that at the moment you need a Google email account to register.

Social media guide, FamilySearch
familysearch.org/learn/wiki/en/Social_Media

Quick guide to the subject, with links to pages that focus on individual social networks and how to use them for genealogy. Meanwhile, the current FamilySearch homepage is geared towards creating an online tree, and the site has incorporated useful networking tools such as MyHeritage's smart/record-matching facility.

GenesReunited
genesreunited.co.uk

The concept of GenesReunited, and its trailblazing parent FriendsReunited, was of course to connect – to network. And like most leading genealogy sites, including its step-sister Findmypast, it encourages you to start by entering your family details into a simple, shareable online tree.

Flickr
flickr.com

Since launch, this photo-sharing and photography-appreciation website has been given social network-style makeovers. You can 'friend' other users, leave comments, send messages, form groups, and integrate photo streams with other social media networks.

FamilyRelatives
familyrelatives.com

The site's new Family Tree allows users to create and build a tree, share and collaborate, match family members and add media files.

Genoom
genoom.com

Social networking platform.

See also: 5.2 Blogs and Forums, 5.7 Sharing Research, 5.9 Software and Apps

5.9 Software and Apps

The market for specialist genealogical software has changed in recent years, as the boundaries between website and software blur as a result of cloud computing solutions, online family trees and a greater emphasis on networking. These sit alongside the increasing numbers of apps for mobile and tablet computers: some are little more than mobile-friendly versions of their parent website, while others are standalone tools for researchers at the coalface.

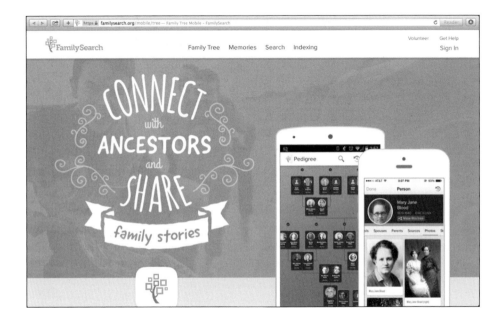

FamilySearch Tree
familysearch.org/mobile/tree

The official FamilySearch mobile companion app to FamilySearch Family Tree (familysearch.org/tree). There's also FamilySearch Memories (familysearch.org/mobile/memories).

RootsMagic
rootsmagic.com/app/

Very popular application, with several variations. This address takes you to the companion mobile app.

WikiTree
wikitree.com

At the time of writing the online tree includes 8,806,843 people contributed by 231,896 genealogists.

RootsMagic App for iOS and Android

Your family tree at your fingertips! Now you can easily take and show off your family history with you wherever you go.

Reunion
leisterpro.com

Often described as one of the best specialist family history programs on the market.

Centenary Connections
centenaryconnections.org

'Journey across Greater Manchester to discover stories of the First World War ...'.

Pic Scanner
appinitio.com / picscanner /

Use your mobile or tablet to scan / digitize old family photographs.

INTERVIEWY
interviewy.co.uk

Mobile voice-recording app – useful for interviewing family members.

WDYTYA? Forum
whodoyouthinkyouaremagazine.com / news / download-our-free-forum-app

Who Do You Think You Are? Magazine's forum spin-off app.

Geneanet
en.geneanet.org

Mobile family tree editor for iPhone and Android.

Families
telgen.co.uk/families/
The Families app works in conjunction with Legacy Family Tree.

Family Tree Maker
familytreemaker.com
The traditional desktop market leader, from ancestry.com.

DropBox
dropbox.com
Popular cloud storage solution.

Geni
geni.com
There's also the allied GeneDroid app.

LiveHistory
livehistoryapp.com
'Genealogy and Biography for iPad.'

Genoom
genoom.com

Ancestry App
ancestry.co.uk/cs/ancestry-app

Findmypast, Capture
findmypast.co.uk/capture

BillionGraves App
billiongraves.com/pages/help/mobiledevice.php

MobileFamilyTree
syniumsoftware.com/mobilefamilytree/

Heredis
heredis.com

TreeView
thegenealogist.co.uk/app/

Europeana Apps
labs.europeana.eu/apps/

History of York in WW1
historyofyork.org.uk/mobile/home.html

Hidden Newcastle
www.hiddennewcastle.org

Building the Titanic
channel.nationalgeographic.com/channel/titanic-100-years/articles/download-the-building-titanic-ipad-app/

US National Archives, Mobile Apps
archives.gov/social-media/mobile-apps.html

Streetmuseum: Londinium
museumoflondon.org.uk/Resources/app/Streetmuseum-Londinium/home.html

Today in History
todayhistory.net

HistoryPin
historypin.org/app

Archives
archives.com

One Great Family
onegreatfamily.com

FamilyLink
familylink.com

FamilyRelatives Family Tree
familyrelatives.com/tree/start.php

Legacy Family Tree
legacyfamilytree.com

MyHeritage App
myheritage.com/myceleb?mode=site

Find a Grave
findagrave.com

GedStar Pro for Android
gedstarpro.com

See also: 1.1 Getting Started, 5.2 Blogs and Forums, 5.7 Sharing Research, 5.8 Social Networking

INDEX